The Two Things that Matter Most

KEITH R. GARDNER

ISBN 978-1-68197-609-9 (Paperback)
ISBN 978-1-68197-610-5 (Digital)

Christian Faith Publishing, Inc.
296 Chestnut Street
Meadville, PA 16335
www.christianfaithpublishing.com

Printed in the United States of America

CONTENTS

PREFACE

Many books have been written about improving oneself, finding success or discovering the happiness within, but few books have a prescription that fits all. With the average life span covering about 29,127 days, where do we invest our time and resources? A recent survey asked the question, "What do you consider to be the most important pursuit in life?" Sixty-one percent of the people responded "having a good moral character." Another 29 percent said "having healthy relationships," while a remaining 10 percent felt that "having a good career and achieving financial independence" were the most important pursuits in life.

Most people would agree that life is the most precious gift we can experience. Life can be exciting, enjoyable, and fulfilling, but life can also be challenging. Not everyone experiences the best that life has to offer. Even with much God-given potential and opportunity in life, participants must be engaged. Another way of saying it is "each of us has a personal responsibility for the outcomes of our lives." Active participation allows us to put the most into life, and it also allows us to get the most out of life as well. We must assess risks, maximize opportunities, and make good decisions if we hope to achieve success. The Bible says, Life is like a vapor that appears for a short time and then vanishes away. How we invest our time is critically important. Evangelist Dr. Billy Graham once said, "In dialogues with young people, many [say that] more than they want things, they want to know how to find meaning and purpose. I suggest they can achieve these desires only when they find three things: a moral code to follow, a cause to serve, and a creed to believe in."[1] As members of the human race, we are created for success. Most people want to find fulfillment and to make a difference in the world. The Bible says, "We are fearfully and wonderfully made," which implies that we have all the creative tools, a divine purpose, and the spiritual resources necessary to reach our God-given potential. If we were to think of life as a bank, we could keep a tally of our personal account by recording the deposits and withdrawals we make in life. There is an old saying, "Life is like money. You can spend it any way you want, but you can only spend it once." The question is, How would you spend yours?

Jesus was once asked about the most important pursuit in life, and He responded, "'You shall love the Lord your God with all your heart, with all your soul, with all your mind, and with all your strength, and the second is like it, you shall love your neighbor as yourself.' There is no other commandment greater than these."[2] If you analyze Jesus's statement carefully, you'll see He reduces the important things in life to just two worthwhile pursuits, to love God and love others. Why would Jesus put such a high value on relationships, rather than personal achievement, especially in a culture that promotes becoming rich and famous, advancing medical science, or championing global climate change? There may not be anything inherently wrong with achieving wealth and fame, finding a cure for cancer, or addressing environmental concerns, but the real answer to the question about what is the most important pursuit in life is that God has made us for relationships. According to Jesus, we are created with a fairly simple mission, "To love God first, and love others!" Throughout the Bible we see the same theme appear over and over again in stories, parables, and biblical teachings. We were created for

---

[1]   Billy Graham, *Reader's Digest* (Harlan: May 2014).
[2]   Mark 12:29–31 (NKJV).

relationships! The Bible is, and will always be, the greatest resource for navigating life's journey. It is our GPS for life! It is my hope this book encourages you to seek and develop the *two things that matter most;* they are the two most important things you'll ever do in life.

Thank you to my wife, Sheryl, for her support and encouragement during the writing of the book and to Dr. Sandra Tawake, for her dedication to the Lord and her unwavering commitment to excellence. Without her oversight and editorial labor, this project would have remained incomplete. And a special 'thanks' to my publisher Christian Faith Publishing, for their patience and assistance in bringing this book to completion and helping it to become what the author had hoped it to be. And the most important "thanks" to Jesus Christ, who has been the Author and Finisher of my faith!

CHAPTER ONE

The Journey

Things That Shape Our Tomorrows

Throughout the course of life you will experience activities and events that help shape your outlook on life. Events will not completely define the person you will become, but they do help shape your attitudes, your perspective, and your priorities in life. An early experience has helped to shape me. As an eleven-year-old boy, in the summer of 1968, I experienced an unexpected and unforeseen tragedy that affected my life and shaped my outlook on both life and death. I experienced the loss of my best friend. As a young boy, I was involved in outdoor activities with friends in my neighborhood.

One of those friends was another eleven-year-old boy named Mark. Mark had been a friend who attended the same elementary school that I did. Our mothers took turns picking us up and dropping us off at school, and Mark was a member of the same Cub Scout pack as I was. Occasionally Mark and I would have a sleepover at each other's homes, and I considered him a BFF, a best friend forever. Mark and I were growing up before video games and electronic gadgetry came on the scene. We spent most of our time playing outdoors with bats and balls and gloves or riding bikes. Our games depended on ingenuity and our imaginations.

We lived near Rock Creek Park, which had a swimming pool, tennis courts, and a softball field. For twenty-five cents we could go to the park and swim all day in the pool. It provided relief from the heat for young kids not accustomed to sitting in air-conditioned houses or buildings. The park was the family's social gathering place and a magnet for the youth.

Innocence and Tragedy

On that hot summer day in 1968 Mark and another friend named Glenn wanted to go to the park to spend the afternoon playing in the pool and at the obstacle course. What happened next put into motion a series of events that shattered our friendship and left an indelible blemish on all of our lives. What affected me most was the tragic way it happened. Most of us were expecting to have at least one or two more trips to the park during the final days of summer. On this day a little before noon Mark had called his mother to ask permission to ride his bike to the park. He told her that he and Glenn would be riding together, and they would be careful. Mark's mother told him to make sure that he obeyed all the safety rules and she would permit him to go. Mark was an exceptionally obedient young boy, and his mother knew he would do as he promised. And with that Mark and Glenn set out from home to ride their bikes to the park. Both lived less than a mile and a half away from the park. The bike ride would take only about six or seven minutes, but on this day they never reached the park.

What happened next defied all logic and any reasonable expectation. According to witnesses as Mark and Glenn rode their bikes to the park, a drunk driver crossed the center line and ran off the left-hand side of the road and crashed into their bikes. Mark and Glenn were five feet off the shoulder of the road, riding legally and obeying all traffic laws when their bikes were struck. The impaired driver was a troubled middle-aged woman. The car she was driving never even slowed down. Glenn was riding his bike on the outside of Mark, farthest from the car when he was hit. He was thrown off his bike, sustaining severe injuries. Mark would later recount that Glenn had been so far off the road that he was surprised that Glenn had been struck. Mark was on the inside, closest to the car. When the car struck Mark, apparently it knocked him and his bike to the ground. Since the driver failed to apply the brakes, Mark's body was pinned under the car momentarily. News reports indicated the driver traveled nearly the distance of a football field before finally stopping the car. The emergency crews were called and responded quickly to transport both Mark and Glenn to the hospital.

Glenn required multiple surgeries on his legs. One leg sustained permanent damage and ended up a couple of inches shorter than the other, so that Glenn required the support of a brace to walk. Mark, however, sustained the worst of the injuries. When Mark reached the operating room, doctors discovered that part of a bone in his arm was missing. Investigators went back to the crash site to retrieve it, and surgeons were able to reinsert it. Mark sustained multiple injuries, both internally and externally. In addition to broken bones, he also suffered a fractured skull. When Mark came out of recovery and regained consciousness, he asked his mother to take him home. She told him as soon as he was a little better she would take him home. Each day Mark asked if he could go home, and each day his mother told him, "As soon as you're a little better, we'll carry you home." On the third day after the accident, he asked again if he could go home, and she said, "Maybe tomorrow we can go home!" He said, "I don't think I'll be here tomorrow, Mom." And almost prophetically, he wasn't. For reasons known only to heaven, his brief life ended in its eleventh year.

Lasting Impression

The life and death of my friend Mark profoundly affected me for a long time. It was nearly thirty years later, when my own mother passed away, that I really began to process the reality and finality of death. After my mother's funeral, I contacted Mark's parents and asked if I could come by for a visit. They lived in the same house they had lived in when I was a boy, so memories invaded me as I drove up the driveway. Mark's mother invited my wife and me into the living room where we sat down. They were extremely gracious in allowing me to come by and share my personal loss. I was hoping Mark's family could help me reconcile life's purposes with life's losses. They gladly received me and my wife in their home, and we spent some time together sharing stories and reminiscing.

We shared memories from thirty years earlier as well as my grief over the recent loss of my mother. Mark's mother told me of a special time that I had not been aware of, a time when my mother had comforted her in the kitchen the day Mark died. My mother had lost a three-year-old son due to a defective heart condition. She shared her personal pain of losing a child in order to comfort Mark's mother. It brought me solace knowing she was willing to share the pain she experienced so others benefited. But I still struggled with the loss of Mark's life when I was eleven and even at fifty-one I need to articulate what our purpose is in life and how to find it and know it.

Two Lessons I Learned

Lesson one is a hard lesson to learn; it is one that takes time to process, mentally and spiritually. Lesson one says, *Even though I may not understand the reasons certain things happen the way they do, I can have confidence that God does.* God works in mysterious ways, and He is all-knowing and all-powerful. Mankind is limited, and we must learn to live with our limitations. God, on the other hand, does not have human limitations. Since He is all-knowing and all-powerful,

He possesses the knowledge that exceeds human thought and understanding. One thing I have come to appreciate experientially is God's overseeing care. God will not allow our hurts to be more than we can bear (although there are times we may be at our limit). He also does not allow our hurts to be wasted. Even if our personal understanding is blurred (which is often the case), God is still sovereign, and He maintains a finger on the pulse of the human race.

Lesson two, I discovered through my own experience, *God is the Potter and we are the clay.* Sometimes God takes the broken pieces of our lives and puts them back together and fashions them in such a way as to make the final product beneficial for other people. In Mark's case, his precious young life could not be replaced. But several things came out of a terrible, terrible tragedy that may not have happened otherwise. Mark's mother became an advocate against drunk driving, as she told her story to others. The number of people she influenced and the countless lives that were saved as a result of her advocacy can not be known. The Governor of North Carolina and the Highway Safety Council sponsored a movie based on Mark's story that highlighted the dangers and the consequences of drunk driving. The movie was distributed to each school sponsoring drivers' education programs, and it became part of the education curriculum for young people seeking a driver's license in the state. The story of a terrible tragedy was turned into a message of accountability and responsibility. The complete impact of that message may not be fully known this side of heaven, but it has made a difference.

Finding Purpose

Many times we come to a crossroads in life where decisions we make have long-lasting consequences. Our dreams and promises intersect with reality and responsibility. It is true, in many cases, that our hopes and dreams for tomorrow are affected by our actions today. Author and pastor John Ortberg recounts an experience he had early in his own life that affected his future outlook. He said, "I am in a state of disappointment. I am missing the life that I was appointed by God to live—missing my calling."[3] He was describing the internal struggle many feel when they reach a crossroads in life and are faced with uncertainty. Many people reevaluating life or entering midlife find themselves along with nearly 20 percent of the population wanting a do-over in life. Captain Chesley "Sully" Sullenberger, the pilot who landed US Airways Flight 1549 on the Hudson River after striking a flock of geese in New York, shares the following observation: "Given the rapid rate of change in today's culture and the constant state of flux in our industries, in our economic system, and in this worldwide marketplace of ideas, it is essential that we try to understand what it means to be an effective leader in the modern world. For me, there is no effective way to cope with the ambiguity and complexity so prevalent today unless one has a clear set of values."[4]

Regardless of our age, gender, or ethnicity, we are programmed to function better with a clear set of values. Values give us purpose and direction in life. They establish a foundation of stability for our hopes and dreams of the future. Values help balance our priorities, and they are at the very core of who we are. Our values influence both our thinking and our motivation and consequently have to be established first before any other choice in life. We will return to the importance of values in just a moment.

An Alarming Statistic
Over the past decade the percentage of unemployed people in the United States (both men and women) sixteen years of age and

---

[3]   John Ortberg et al., *The Life You've Always Wanted* (Grand Rapids: Zondervan Publishers, 2002), 14.

[4]   Chesley Sullenberger, *Making a Difference* (New York: HarperCollins Publishers, 2012), 4.

older has been 6.5 percent. This may not be a number that grabs our attention or sounds very alarming, but when you consider there are 36,902 men and 49,724 women not factored in because they have left the workforce, it is sobering. Even more staggering, the unemployment rate for young men and women sixteen to nineteen years of age was 19.1 percent with a participation rate of only 33.2 percent.[5] At a time when they should be seeking career goals, developing strategies for successful living, and finding direction in life, today's young people are finding life a bit challenging.

On a more positive note, in a recent survey of working people ranging in ages from twenty to sixty years of age, people were asked, "Would you consider your outlook on life to be pessimistic, optimistic, philosophical, or theological?" Nearly 60 percent of those persons surveyed responded their outlook was optimistic despite economic challenges and difficulties they were facing. The Barna Group research showed that three-quarters of US adults (75 percent) say they are looking for ways to live a more meaningful life—whether such meaning is found in family, career, church, projects, or life choices.[6] In order words, 75 percent of US adults are reassessing their value systems and looking for ways to have a more meaning in life. They are searching for ways to leave a bigger footprint for others to follow.

Seeking a Value System

It seems that every generation has an inherent expectation from people who are born into it. Our lives are shaped from infancy to adulthood by factors both internal and external. Much of our early development is shaped by circumstances and situations that we are

[5]   *US Bureau of Labor Statistics*, accessed on May 23, 2014, http://bls.gov/cgi-bin.
[6]   Barna Group, "The Trends on Faith, Work and Calling," accessed May 23, 2014, http://barna.org.

born into that are beyond our control. We do not choose the families we are born into. We have no say in our early economic situation, nor do we vote on the career paths that our parents or caretakers follow. We are affected, by the decisions they have made. Their decisions, good or bad, ultimately become the building blocks for our own lives.

It is interesting, however, that we are born into a world of dependence. By its very nature, dependence requires us to become takers rather than givers. As we mature, though, our lives must be transformed by growth and development into independence. That is how society is structured. It is necessary to establish a clear set of values early to guide us in our development. Values will point us toward choosing our cause, our creed, and our code, and they will ultimately determine where we end up. We must transition from codependence into independence. Our experiences and our relationships with others are part of the growth process. They provide us with the prime motivation for life. Motivation is from the root word *motive*, which means "an emotion, a desire, a physiological need, or similar impulse acting as an incitement to action."[7] Our motivation for life and our ability to establish a goal or fulfill a dream requires one critical thing from us: the development of a healthy *attitude*.

Attitude Is to Life What an Arrow Is to a Bow

Motivational speaker Zig Ziglar once said, "You already have every characteristic necessary for success. It's your attitude, not your aptitude, that determines our altitude."[8] Developing the right attitude is critical in determining and reaching our expectations in life.

---

[7]   *The American Heritage Dictionary*, 2nd ed. (Boston: Houghton Mifflin Co. 1985), 817.

[8]   Successories, *Great Quotes from Zig Ziglar* (Franklin Lakes: Career Press, 1997), 11.

Our attitude is the mental disposition or state of mind developed from the physical, the emotional, and the intellectual and spiritual experiences of life. Attitude is to life what an arrow is to a bow. A bow without an arrow is rendered useless and keeps an archer from being effective or successful. Our attitude contributes significantly to the process of evaluating the challenges of life and implementing a strategy for success. The Old Testament provides insight into early biblical thinkers' ideas about attitude. "For as he [mankind] thinks in his heart, so is he" (Proverbs 7:23). This author's translation: "We are the total sum of what we think of ourselves and what we choose to surround ourselves with."

Our attitude can be, and often is, just as important as our behavior. For instance, a bad attitude is a tip off to future bad behavior. Pouting, sulking, scowling, deep sighing, and slamming doors are all indicators of a sour attitude. We all know how devastating a bad attitude can be. We have seen it in our sports heroes, our co-workers, our business associates, and even in our families. The great theologian and Bible teacher Matthew Henry was once robbed of all of his money by some thieves. That night he sat down in a hotel room and wrote these words in his diary:

I am so very thankful.
1. First of all, because I was never robbed before.
2. Second, because although they took my money, they did not take my life.
3. Third, because although they took all the money I had, it wasn't very much.
4. Fourth, it was I who was robbed, not I who robbed.[9]

---

[9] Matthew Henry, *Prayer of Thanks* Online.matthew-henry-prayer-of-thanks. (accessed 5/30/2014).

Many people admire the type of attitude expressed by Henry. It is an attitude shaped through the process of adversity through life's experiences. It is the type of attitude we ought to incorporate into our own lives if we are to be successful. It is an attitude of being thankful for what we've been blessed with, rather than being dissatisfied over missing out on what we think we deserve.

Shaping of Our Attitudes

It is quite normal for people to rise to the occasion when faced with big challenges, or to fall flat on their faces when confronted with obstacles. Having the right attitude and nurturing that attitude will affect the way we view the world. We need to remember we are not a product of our circumstances entirely. We are a product of the attitude that we allow to develop around those circumstances. We have choices in life, and we are the ones who ultimately determine our choices, how we view them, and whether we are going to take advantage of our opportunities. We can see the glass half full, or we can see the glass half empty. Our internal and external perception and our intellectual evaluation will determine the power and strength of our attitude. Having a strong positive attitude is a powerful motivator in accomplishing short-range and long-range goals. *It's your attitude, not your aptitude, that will determine your altitude.*

Choosing Wisely

While our attitudes control our perspective on life and determine the way we approach our individual challenges, we ultimately decide through the decision-making process which direction to go. One of the greatest gifts we have in America is the ability to choose our outcomes and determine our own futures. As human beings, we choose how we want to incorporate our talents, our abilities, and our education. We can place special emphasis on things that interest us, like our educational pursuits or special trainings. Or we can pursue our own natural bent in life; another way of saying natural bent is "the way we roll." It's worth noting, choice is a two-sided coin. The negative side of choice is we also can choose to allow those same interests, pursuits, and opportunities to lie dormant, undeveloped, and underutilized. That choice represents a failure to pursue God-given abilities, special or natural gifts, and talents that a person is born with. When this happens, it leads to a disappointing lifestyle, accepting what is least rather than choosing what is best.

In his book *Living above the Level of Mediocrity*, Chuck Swindoll used a reprint of a motivational phrase from United Technologies that offers this encouragement:

> The greatest waste of our natural resources is the number of people who never achieve their potential. Get out of that slow lane. Shift into that fast lane. If you think you can, there's a good chance you will. Even making the effort will make you feel like a new person. Reputations are made by searching for things that can't be done and doing them.
>
> Aim low: *boring.* Aim high: *soaring.*[10]

Sadly, some people do not wish to reach their full potential, and they are threatened by others who do. They can be discouraging, and they usually contribute to a negative environment, critical of people who do. An old Chinese proverb says, "The person who says it can't be done should not interrupt the person doing it." Part of the decision-making process is to surround yourself with people who encourage you rather than discourage you.

---

[10] Charles R. Swindoll, *Living Above the Level of Mediocrity* (Dallas: Word Publishing, 1987), 9.

Rejecting Failure

One often overlooked aspect of the decision-making process is fear; one must not *be afraid of failure*. Failure does not have to be fatal. Failure simply means that a particular path is not the most direct path to your success. Many lessons can be learned in the process of striving to succeed that become value tools in the process of building a life.

Someone once asked the late Paul Harvey, the journalist and radio commentator, to reveal the secret of his success, and his response was "I get up when I fall down." Not everyone will be successful the first time one tries something. When one falls down, one must get back up.

Rejection and failure are common components of life, and everyone will face one or the other or both at some point. We should be encouraged rather than discouraged because rejection and/or failure can act as motivation for our successes if we recognize them and handle them properly. We sometimes refer to it as constructive criticism or constructive review. Consider the following story as a good example.

Author Neil Postman tells a humorous story of a letter written by a high school senior who had received a letter of rejection from the college he wanted to attend. His response shows the power of determination and the necessity of rejecting rejection. "Dear Admissions Officer," the student wrote, "I am in receipt of your rejection of my application. As much as I would like to accommodate you, I find I cannot accept it. I have already received four rejections from other colleges, and this number is, in fact, over my limit. Therefore, I must reject your rejection and will appear for classes on Sept. 18."[11] We may

---

[11] Neil Postman, *Conscientious Objections: Stirring Up Trouble About Language, Technology and Education* (New York: Knopf. First Vintage Book Edition, 1988).

never know what circumstance the student found when he appeared for classes on September 18, but I sense that whatever his circumstance, he was prepared to handle it with ample determination. In life, you will be served well if you have a healthy dose of "determination" as part of your personality and general demeanor. Your job applications, promotions, special certifications, or ideas may get rejected initially. But remember *rejection is not fatal.* Rejection simply means that your product or your idea is not yet ready for human consumption. In fact, rejection can strengthen resolve to be successful by increasing the level of determination. Many have risen from failure to achieve real success by rejecting the rejection of the world.

- In 1902, the poetry editor of *The Atlantic Monthly* returned a sheaf of poems to a twenty-eight-year-old poet with this curt note: "Our magazine has no room for your vigorous verse." The poet was Robert Frost, who became one of the great poets of the twentieth century; he rejected the rejection.
- In 1905, the University of Bern turned down a PhD dissertation as being irrelevant and fanciful. The young physics student who wrote the dissertation was Albert Einstein, who rejected the rejection.
- In 1894, the rhetoric teacher at Harrow in England wrote on the sixteen-year-old's report card, "a conspicuous lack of success." The sixteen-year-old was Winston Churchill, who rejected the rejection and later inspired his country to victory over Hitler's Germany by saying, "Never give up. Never, never, give up."
- Consider the spray lubricant WD-40. *WD-40* literally stands for *Water Displacement, 40th formula.* That's the name straight out of the lab book used by the chemist who developed the product back in 1953. The chemist,

Norm Larsen, was attempting to concoct a formula to prevent corrosion—a task which is done by displacing water. Norm's persistence paid off when he perfected the formula on his fortieth try.[12] That explains why the product is not called WD-25 or WD-30. The chemist, Norm Larsen, would simply not accept failure as being fatal.

A Basic Building Block

It has been said, "In order to know where you're going, you need to know where you've been." The same is true in life. In order to be successful and know where you're going, you need to have a good idea of where you've been. The history of your existence is a key component of what makes you human. You may have all the desire of your heart to fly like a bird or to swim like a fish, but if that is not part of your natural history, certain modifications will be required. Part of the research for this book was to locate a starting point for our self-evaluation. This author was particularly interested in finding out what most people believed about the origin of life. C. S. Lewis once said, "If there is no intelligence behind the universe, then nobody designed my brain for the purpose of thinking. Thought is merely the byproduct of some atoms within my skull. But if so, how can I trust my own thinking to be true? And if I can't trust my own thinking, of course, I can't trust arguments leading to atheism and therefore have no reason to be an atheist, or anything else. Unless I believe in God, I can't believe in thought; so I can never use thought to disbelieve God."[13] What we believe about the origin of life determines our perspective on life in general and how we approach it.

---

12   "Frequently Asked Questions," WD-40 Company, accessed February 14, 2015, http.//wd40.com/faqs.

13   C. S. Lewis, *Broadcast Talks* (London: 1946), 37; quoted in David Noebel, *Understanding the Times* (Harvest House, 1994), p. 93.

A survey was developed in research for this book to lay a foundation of understanding for the author. One of the survey questions asked, "When considering your own personal conviction concerning the origin of life, what do you believe?" The four choices were evolution, special creation, a combination of evolution and special creation, or the truth is still unknown. Nearly 62 percent of the people responding to the survey believed in special creation as the starting point for life. Another 24 percent believed in a combination of special creation and evolution, while only 9 percent believed in evolution. This result was surprising, given the educational promotion of evolution in the curriculum in the public school systems nationwide. The remaining 5 percent felt the truth of creation is still unknown.

An interesting fact regarding the origin of life is, regardless of what you believe or consider fact, your belief is based on faith. There is no scientific evidence that is conclusive for belief system, evolution, or creation. Everyone's conclusions about what they believe are based solely on faith. Whether you are a believer, an atheist, or an agnostic, what you accept as evidence is based on your own particular educational emphasis. Most people in the survey leaned toward belief in special creation as having the greater compelling argument for their origin. Almost every civilization that has ever existed has at least some innate sense of a supreme being. Even remote tribes from every corner of the globe had a belief in some type of supreme being responsible for the origin of life, great spirits or angels, or sun and moon gods. The concept of being finite and limited while being faced with the infinite and unexplainable seems to suggest something larger at work in the world. With only conscience and intellect in play, everything we see in our universe suggests organization. Order and structure undeniably abound in nature, in the cosmos, and even in our own physiological system.

Considering Observable Science

When one considers the complexity of the human body with everything so delicately arranged, one is instantly made aware of order and precision. It is easy to draw the conclusion with simple deductive methods that someone or something greater than human intelligence is responsible for human existence. It is the only reasonable explanation that makes sense if we consider the function of our own bodies. Our hearts beat with regularity, pumping the life blood, forcing nutrients and oxygen through the organs of our bodies in order to sustain life. The liver, kidneys, bladder, lungs, and other organs process nutrients into energy; they cleanse the blood of waste and provide oxygen to limbs and muscles with each organ providing a special function in giving life. All of these processes happen in an organized and coordinated manner. Medical science has learned to duplicate and replicate many of these individual processes in the body. Medical science can prolong life, but it cannot create life. Medical science falls short of having all of the processes synchronized so they work in concert together in sustaining life.

If that were not enough, look into the sky at the cosmos with all of our advancements in science. We are able to see all of the order and structure that has been orchestrated throughout the universe. If we consider the orbiting of planets, the gravitational pull that establishes balance throughout the universe, and the rotating of planets on axes, it would be hard to imagine this simply happening as the result of billions of years of things haphazardly floating around in space and ultimately arranging themselves in an orderly flow. The only plausible explanation is the presence of what we can only identify as an infinite supreme being, a supreme being far above human capabilities and human science. The Bible affirms this observation in Psalm 19:1: "The heavens declare the glory of God; and the firmament shows His handiwork."[14]

---

[14]   Psalm 19:1 (NKJV).

THE TWO THINGS THAT MATTER MOST

Science and faith both cry out for an intelligent Master Designer, One who is infinite in wisdom and abilities, exceeding mankind's finite limitations and understanding, and One who is referred to and known characteristically as *God*.

Why Is This Important?

If there is order in the world and structure in our human existence, then life is more than just a cosmic haphazard series of celestial events. We can rightly assume that life has a Creator and the Creator has a plan. If there is an orchestrated series of events with a Creator and a plan, we can safely assume we are a part of the plan.

Author and pastor Lee Strobel points out his book *The Case for a Creator*, "You'll soon find that the universe is governed by both physical laws and spiritual laws. The physical laws point us toward the Creator; the spiritual laws tell us how we can know him personally, both today and forever. After all, he's not just the Creator in a broad sense; he's your Creator. You were created to relate to him in a vibrant, dynamic, and intimate way. And if you seek him wholeheartedly, he promises to provide all the clues you need to find him."[15] In our search for purpose we looked for clues to direct our paths and guide us toward things that are of special interest.

Each person has a uniqueness that makes him/her different from every other person who has ever lived, and that uniqueness is the special identity each has as part the human race. Just like snowflakes and fingerprints have a uniqueness which makes them similar but different, each of us is unique. This personal uniqueness makes a special one-of-a-kind person. There is only one "you," and there will always be only one "you." Since you cannot be duplicated or repli-

---

[15]   Lee Strobel, *The Case for a Creator* (Grand Rapids, MI: Zondervan, 2004), 291–292.

cated, it's very important to make your life count and fulfill the plan that God has designed for your life.

What the Bible Says!

The Bible tells us of our origin and purpose in life in Genesis 1:26–27: "Then God said, 'Let Us make man in Our image, according to Our likeness; let them have dominion over the fish of the sea, over the birds of the air, and over the cattle, over all the earth and over every creeping thing that creeps on the earth.' So God created man in His [own] image; in the image of God He created him; male and female He created them."[16] This passage reveals that life is no accident or series of inadvertent cosmic processes. You and I were created for a specific purpose with godly expectations. This was the beginning of a relationship God initiated by creating mankind. This act of creation was not something God had to do. God chose creation out of His divine will of love. God's divine purpose was to have fellowship through a relationship with the crowning jewel of His creation—mankind.

The Bible teaches that life is a gift from God and mankind is made in His image. Within its pages the Bible provides instruction from God on how we are to make life count. We are told Christ came "to give life and to give it more abundantly." In other words, Christ came so we might live life to its fullest extent. The Bible also says: "Ask and it will be given to you, seek and you shall find, knock and the door will be opened."[17] What a great invitation from the Creator of life to simply ask, seek, or knock and we can have an answer and a response to life. With such a wonderful offer, though, it's puzzling that so many people fail. Why do so many people fail to achieve life's

---

16   Genesis 1:26–27 (NKJV).
17   Matthew 7:7 (NKJV).

best? What holds us back from succeeding in life? What are the barriers that prevent people from being all God planned?

We Are Being Culturally Conditioned For a Low Bar

Values and culture norms of society have declined steadily over the past fifty years. History records a time when exceptionalism, hard work, commitment, dedication, and doing the right thing were qualities that were admired by all Americans. Today in our postmodern culture the norm is to place everyone on the same economic and cultural level. Equality is the new clarion call for society; everyone should be equal in every respect; despite obvious differences. Rather than appreciating differences that exist and celebrating them, society is engaged in social engineering. In some respects, government representatives see their roles as agents responsible for transforming America, rather than allowing God to do it. Even though God created everyone with differences, the government is recreating a society where everyone is equal. Despite obvious personal differences in abilities, talents, gifts, gender, race, and ethnicity, as God originally intended, the push is for cultural equality.

With the loss of American exceptionalism, the unintended consequence is a failure of citizens to take personal responsibility for their lives. We are becoming dependent rather than responsible. The result is the dismantling of ideas and personal dreams for citizens and adjusting the attainment bar to a lower, reachable standard for everyone. The term we used to hear in high school was "grading on the curve." Now society seeks to give everyone a perfect score, whether it is deserved or not. The unintended consequences lower the standard for everyone, eliminating motivation and drive. We substitute complacency and contentment for personal motivation and effort, and the end result is a deficiency in our drive to be our best. Unfortunately, this type of system devalues individual God-given abilities and suppresses the uniqueness each of us was created with. Instead of being empowered to dream and reach for the stars, we settle for being enabled and satisfied with just touching earth. This type of conclusion begs the question, "Can't I decide for myself, don't I have a voice?" The answer is "Yes!" Read on.

CHAPTER TWO

If My Life Belongs to Me, Don't I Own it?

We do have ownership of our lives, but we have a shared responsibility with God for what takes place over the course of our lives. Anything meaningful in life will require work, determination, and general sense of direction. Dr. Tony Alessandra says there's an old saying: "Most people aim at nothing in life...and hit it with amazing accuracy." It's a sad commentary about people, but it's true. It is the striving for and the attainment of goals that make life meaningful to the entire generation. Lewis Carroll illustrates this point beautifully in *Alice in Wonderland*:

> ALICE: Mr. Cat, which of these paths shall I take?
> CHESHIRE CAT: Well, my dear, where do you want to go?
> ALICE: I don't suppose it really matters.
> CHESHIRE CAT: Then, my dear, any path will do!

No matter what kind of path you are traveling, whether it's through life or across the country by car, if you don't know where you're going, you'll never know if you've arrived. Knowing where you want to go in life is critical to getting there. Another point that should be made: Taking just any road leaves fulfillment to chance. Having a goal with a destination in mind is essential if one hopes to succeed in life. People who have no goals are normally emotionally, socially, spiritually, physically, and professionally unbalanced. The result can be a tremendous amount of pressure causing personal anxiety. On the other hand, people who have goals are generally respected by their peers. Having the ability and making decisions that affect the direction of life is clearly a sign of strength. Goals create drive, motivation, and direction which definitely affect personality.[18]

Developing an effective plan for life requires an understanding of who you are, where you would like to go, and what you hope to accomplish. Three-time Super Bowl champion and three-time NASCAR champion Joe Gibbs provides helpful insight:

> I have thought a lot about life—what is it? Life to me is a game, and you and I are the players. God is our Head Coach, and no one wants to lose in the biggest game of all…
>
> You and I are playing the most important contest of all. All my experience in leading men— as a coach and team builder—has convinced me that to win a game you need a game plan.[19]

---

[18] Tony Alessandra, "Most People Aim at Nothing in Life…and Hit It with Amazing Accuracy," accessed February 23, 2014, http://www.alessandra.com/freeresources/peopleaim_article.asp.

[19] Joe Gibbs, *Game Plan for Life* (Illinois: Tyndale House Publishers, 2009), 5.

According to Coach Gibbs, having a game plan for life is essential if you hope to be successful in life. The truth is it is possible to exist without having a plan, but you cannot experience real victory in life without one, nor will you be successful. Existing and living are two separate things when it comes to making your life count. Developing a plan with God's help is critical to the success you hope to experience. Having a plan helps gauge your progress in life and provides focus for the challenges that you face.

In our survey to determine how people thought about future success, we asked, "How important is it for you to leave a legacy to others?" Surprisingly, less than 25 percent of those surveyed felt it was one of the most important pursuits in life. Approximately 17 percent of the people did not feel that it was very important at all. Another 58 percent felt that it was only somewhat important. With less than 25 percent of the population focused on making life count, we confront the reality that most people do not think about future success. How can we transform this attitude?.

How Do I Make a Plan?

Most people are not fully aware that a plan already exists for their lives. God, as Creator, has created us according to His own unique plan that takes account of our strengths and weaknesses. We are told in the Bible, "For I know the plans I have for you, declares the Lord, plans to prosper you and not to harm you, plans to give you hope and a future."[20] As both Author and Finisher of our faith, God has deposited a unique plan into every individual He created. God's hope is that we join with Him to experience the very best life has to offer. Since we are finite beings, there is no way we can know everything we need to know in order to achieve success. God, on the other hand, is all-knowing and all-powerful. He has the ability to know our

---

[20]   Jeremiah 29:11 (TNIV).

needs in advance and prepare us for the future. We cannot outthink God, outstrategize God, outmaneuver God or outplan God. God is omniscient, meaning all-knowing; and He is omnipotent, meaning all-powerful, and omnipresent, meaning exists everywhere. God has our best interest at heart, but just a little caveat! God does not force His will or His plan on us. God enters our lives through invitation. We must invite God into our lives through prayer and willingly follow His plan. God's plan requires us to submit ourselves, both to His will and His direction. In other words, we must surrender our plan, in preference to His plan.

What's the Problem?

When you were born, you were created by God having both a body and a soul. In other words, we have a physical nature (our human body) and a spiritual nature (our inner soul). Each nature is designed so it has the capability to respond directly to God at any given time. From a purely human perspective, our physical bodies operate in the here and now with emotions, physical impulses, and our five senses—sight, hearing, taste, touch, and smell. In God's economy we have been given structure for life. The Bible highlights in the Old Testament moral laws, like the Ten Commandments, articulating a code of self-awareness and responsibility. God established governments to administer those moral laws in society. Government is one of three divine institutions ordained by God. The first institution is the family. Second is government. The third institution ordained by God is the Church. God intended all three of these institutions for the structure of society and the organization of life.

The primary problem we have is not with the institutions developed and ordained by God. The primary problem we have as individuals is our own selfish *will*. We want what we want when we want it. We want to go for the gusto, grab the brass ring, and pursue ideas that bring personal gratification. The greatest hindrance to success will not be other people. It will not be lack of opportunity, and it will not be lack of resources or funding. The greatest hindrance to success will be the desire to follow selfish will. We live in a world that offers instant everything. Instant coffee, instant tea, drive-thru windows, microwave ovens, instant communications, iPhones, iPads, and worldwide data collection devices that satisfy every craving and provide instant information. We are lured into a trap that we create. We design it, and we provide the bait. We fall into the snare of self-will and self-absorption. We transport ourselves to the center of the universe, and the unintended consequence is displacing God and cutting off communication with Him. God and His created purpose for our lives become abstract notions, like the hopes of a distant parent or a relative far away.

What Can Be Done?

God has also created mankind with a brain and the ability to distinguish between good and bad. Within that brain resides a spiritual conscience that acts as an internal GPS directing our thoughts and our actions. God created us to be responsible and accountable. Since the Garden of Eden, Satan has operated in stealth-like fashion, influencing decision-making in the lives of both men and women. The Bible refers to Satan as "the prince of this world."[21] This term implies a powerful influence in the world and over society in general. A number of people choose to dismiss a negative spiritual influence in the world despite the good and the evil that exists. The evil that occurs is explained through political correctness. Society refers to dysfunctional families, corruptive influences in life, a defective gene to explain evil. While these forces are present in human life they are the symptoms rather than the root cause of evil.

---

[21]   John 12:31 (NKJV).

The root of our problem is the issue of sin and our selfish desire to fulfill our own personal will. Mankind has been at war with sin since the beginning of time. Sin has sought to deceive, alter, and change our value system since it was introduced into the world. Society has mocked it, marginalized it, and minimized it since its inception in the Garden of Eden. When our attempts to mitigate the results of sin fail, we simply began using our intellectual ability to change the vocabulary. If we strategically change our word usage to more politically correct language, perhaps the problems of society will not be so bad. The major problem with that line of thinking is that we can change the label on a bottle of poison, but it is still poison. If we are not careful how we handle it, it does not matter what is on the label, it still kills. We may try to change its appearance to make it look like something different, but if the contents are still the same, they yield devastating results. The same is true of sin. We can call sin anything else but sin, but it does not diminish the results. It simply makes it more socially acceptable, which lowers our defenses and dulls any awareness of danger.

What Is Sin?

The Bible uses the word *sin* repeatedly from Genesis to Revelation, but society has sought to eliminate it from the English language. Sin in some circles is considered "hate" speech and one who refers to sin today is often castigated as being out of touch. The major problem with sin is that we all are infected by it. The Bible says, "For *all* have sinned and fall short of the glory of God."[22] The Bible's use of the word *all* is inclusive. It covers every single person who has ever lived. No one is excluded, and everyone is infected. Sin is from the Greek word *hamartia* which literally means "to miss the

---

[22]   Romans 3:23 (NKJV).

mark." It is the most comprehensive term for moral obliquity.[23] Sin is not necessarily a violation of civil law or judicial law, although it can be. Sin is a violation of God's moral code of righteousness and results in mankind missing the mark of God's standard.

The root of mankind's fundamental problem is the propensity to sin. Sin is seductive and alluring, but it is also destructive and dangerous. When we become self-absorbed with a desire to satisfy our personal appetites, we will lose our spiritual equilibrium. People who seek to fulfill the desires of the flesh feed their own impulses and fall prey to outside spiritual influences that seek to control their lives. The Bible tells us how sin germinates in our lives: "But each one is tempted when he is drawn away by his own desires and enticed. Then, when desire has conceived, it gives birth to sin; and sin, when it is full-grown, brings forth death."[24] Note the progression of sin in our lives. It begins with an idea or a desire within our hearts. We spend time nurturing it in our minds and thinking how pleasing and pleasurable it might be in reality. We then give birth to it in our thought processes and start taking steps to fulfill our plans in reality.

Why Is This Important to Me?

As the Creator of everything that exists, God has both the right and the prerogative to establish a standard for all of creation, including mankind. In order to make mankind aware of His standard, God communicated it through revelation from Old Testament prophets, in the person of Jesus Christ, through New Testament prophets, and through the Holy Spirit. These revelations culminated in the writing of the most important love letter that has ever been written—the Bible. Norman Geisler and Ron Brooks point out, "The Bible has

---

[23]   W.E. Vine, *Vine's Complete Expository Dictionary of Old and New Testament Words* (Nashville: Thomas Nelson Publishers, 1996), 576.

[24]   James 1:14–15 (NKJV).

many faces. It can be studied as literature and explored as a set of stories and poetic expressions, or viewed as history which tells of the beginnings and growth of God's people...It is God's message to a rebelling world of how it can return to Him."[25]

Jesus made a statement in the Gospel of John that highlights the differences of two competing plans for life. He contrasts the plans by saying, "The thief does not come except to steal, and to kill, and to destroy. I have come that they may have life, and that they may have it more abundantly."[26] Christ is referring to two separate and competing plans for mankind in the physical and spiritual realm. One plan comes from a source that seeks to steal, kill, and destroy, offering temporary pleasure, indulgence, and enjoyment and gratification of self-will.

I have seen the first plan experientially in the life of my mother. My mother was the cheerleader of my life as I grew up. She was protective and supportive of all that my sister, my brother, and I did. She supported us in playing sports, PTA meetings, working outside the home to provide a better living for us, and supporting us educationally. I remember on one occasion my mother going to the school and talking with my teacher and promising to work with me over the course of the summer if the teacher promised not to fail me in the third grade. Back then, failing a grade had a stigma attached to it that my mother did not want me to experience, so she intervened and kept her promise.

The thief came later in life and offered my mother a plan of indulgence and a way to escape pressures in life by promising pleasures through alcohol consumption. Over a period of a dozen years my mother became an alcoholic. During that time I sought to inter-

---

25   Norman Geisler and Ronald Brooks, *When Skeptics Ask* (Grand Rapids: Baker Books, 1996), 141.

26   John 10:10 (NKJV).

vene and rescue her from her addiction only to be told on one occasion I was "no longer her son." At the age of fifty-one, my mother died from cirrhosis of the liver. The thief had come to steal, kill, and destroy. Sadly enough, the thief brought his plan to fruition in our family. He successfully stole my mother's life through alcohol, wrecked our family relationships, and destroyed the family unit. He accomplished his purpose by blinding her from truth, telling her a lie, and getting her to believe it. Satan's lie is always the same, promising to fulfill everyone's goals and make life better and more enjoyable, but the end result is predictable. Sin *always* leads to heartache, heartbreak, and disappointment.

Jesus Christ offers another plan for life. His plan promises "to give life and to give it more abundantly." This scripture refers not to eternal life but to life in the here and now. It speaks of giving life purpose, vitality, and fulfillment. It means making life count and even exceeding one's own expectations. The word *abundantly* in this passage means "existing or occurring in large amounts, marked by great plenty."[27] Obviously, Christ intends a plan that exceeds human ability and achievement, a plan rooted in God's provision and His specific design for our individual lives, a godly plan with our greatest good at heart, providing all the resources necessary to achieve personal success and lead us to an abundant life God has planned for us. Without question, this plan is the better of the two.

How Do I Respond?

We shape responses to our physical nature through education, life experiences, and interactions with other people. If we desire a certain career in life—such as being a doctor, a lawyer, or a teacher—we may seek higher education from a college or university in order

---

[27] *Merriam-Webster Online Dictionary*, s.v. "abundant," accessed February 15, 2014, http://www.merriam-webster.com/dictionary/abundantly.

to attain our goal. Life experiences shape the way we look at life and help frame the attitudes we develop. Interacting with others on a regular basis will help develop personal skill sets that are fundamental in building relationships.

We respond to our spiritual nature through faith and belief. Responding to our physical and spiritual natures can be equally important. The physical and spiritual natures are designed to work together in concert with each other to help us reach our full potential. We all have a vested interest in how life works and what avenues we follow to be successful in life. The most fundamental approach you or I could have in making life count is to research and develop God's plan for our lives. With the Bible being our navigational device for life, God has given both general and specific instructions to follow.

For instance, many Proverbs were handed down from God to Solomon and to other early biblical writers. It was Solomon who asked God for wisdom, and the result was many short Old Testament writings known as Proverbs. Proverbs are succinct, pithy sayings that express timeless truths and project insightful wisdom. They often arrest the thoughts and ideas of the individual causing the reader to reflect on how one might apply divine principles to life situations. For instance, consider Proverbs 3:1–6:

> My son, do not forget my law, but let your heart keep my commands; for length of days and long life and peace they will add to you.
>
> Let not mercy and truth forsake you; bind them around your neck, write them on the tablet of your heart, and so find favor and high esteem in the sight of God and man.
>
> Trust in the Lord with all your heart, and lean not on your own understanding.

In all your ways acknowledge Him, and He
shall direct your paths.

In this passage the wisdom that is passed on to the reader reveals that God has established perimeters in life. We can call it structure, we can call it commands, but the Book of Proverbs calls it law. The law was established to give mankind a system of order that prioritizes human considerations.

Each person born is born as a unique human being. God does not make Xerox copies or clones; He makes only originals. Whether you are a plumber, a preacher, an electrician, an evangelist, a mechanic, or a missionary, God has a specific plan for you, and He wants to guide your every step. This passage in Proverbs 3:1–6 is designed to show the wisdom of aligning one's priorities with God and allowing God to direct each individual path. If God is responsible for your life on planet earth, then He is also responsible for the lives of other people as well. It seems reasonable to expect He would put a plan in place that chooses to maximize existence and to make each individual life count. We see that effort coming out of the wisdom of Proverbs 3. We should seek to do everything to make our lives affect the world in positive ways, but we must never lose sight of the fact that we have a Creator who guides our steps.

Another good example of God directing our steps and helping us prioritize life comes from the Psalmist in the Old Testament where he asks God, "Teach us to number our days that we may gain a heart of wisdom."[28] The idea is that human life is relatively short compared to eternity. People need to prioritize the important things in life in order to maximize their opportunities. The Apostle James makes the same point in the New Testament in the Book of James 4:14: "What is your life? It is even a vapor that appears for a little

---

[28]   Psalm 90:12 (NKJV).

43

time and then vanishes away." What's at stake is the issue of life passing by so quickly that one fails to take advantage of God's provisions.
In fact, the Apostle James goes on to frame the issue with the right
perspective in the next verse: "Instead you ought to say, 'If the Lord
wills, we shall live and do this or that.'"[29] This advice once again,
brings us back to seeking God's will and what He would have us do
rather than seeking our own personal gratification or indulgences in
life. We are created with a specific purpose and plan in life. Finding
that purpose and integrating that purpose with our personal will is
the topic of our next chapter.

---

[29]   James 4:15 (NKJV).

Chapter Three

Is There Purpose in Life?

Seeking to Know Our Purpose

Drawing on one of the most insightful passages in the Bible, I would like for you to see an important principle. Solomon, who historically was proclaimed to be the wisest man who ever lived, gave some of the greatest advice ever heard, and we touched on it in the previous chapter. "Trust in the Lord with all your heart, and lean not on your own understanding; in all your ways acknowledge Him, and He shall direct your paths" (Prov. 3:5–6). Now, there are two parts to this passage that stand out even to the casual Bible reader. First, there is our part. "Trust in the Lord with all your heart, and lean not on your own understanding." Our part of this biblical equation consists of trusting. It is suspending our own intellectual will and desire in preference for God's will and desire for us. It is "unnaturally" reprioritizing what we humanly want and desire and seeking what God wants and desires for us.

I use the word *unnaturally* because our natural desire is to follow our own self-interest and desires. It takes a decision and a strong act of the will to place any considerations before our own. When we

45

seek God's will rather than our own, it transfers our personal motivational drive for life to a higher consideration than simply serving ourselves. It is essentially saying, My human capacity to completely know what's best in life is limited by my finite knowledge and understanding of life. This does not mean we cannot carve out a pathway in life or pursue our own interest. It simply means we cannot know, beyond a shadow of doubt, what is best in life. There are many possibilities in life, and we cannot know every possible outcome. This type of reprioritizing may fall into the category of easier said than done, but we must remember we are not seeking an easy answer. We are seeking the best answer for our circumstances. The best will always be what God intended for us originally. The simple fact we are created in His image suggests we have a higher purpose than simply existing, and only God knows our ultimate purpose. His desire is to put us on the right track so that we have the greatest opportunity for success. Our responsibility is to *trust* in the Lord!

The second part of the equation is what God does. God's part consists of guiding and directing for which He is perfectly suited because He created us, and He knows all of life's possibilities. Author C. S. Lewis once wrote of life's possibilities and likened them to roads. He said, "We are not living in a world where all roads are radii of a circle and where all, if followed long enough, will therefore draw gradually nearer and finally meet at the centre: rather in a world where every road, after a few miles, forks into two, and each of those into two forks again, and at each fork you must make a decision. Even on the biological level life is not like a pool but like a tree. It does not move toward unity but away from it and the creatures grow further apart as they increase in perfection." Lewis goes on to say, "I do not think that all who choose wrong roads perish; but their rescue consists in being put back on the right road. A wrong sum can be put right: but only by going back till you find the error and working it afresh from that point, never by simply going on."[30]

The point that C.S. Lewis makes about life is life is a series of decisions and each decision has its own consequence. Each decision carries the traveler further down a path where sooner or later another decision must be made. Everything may seem fine as long as correct decisions are made. But if the wrong decision is made, it may carry us further from our destination.

An all-knowing God is aware of all of life's possibilities in advance. We have at our disposal His resources, and we can use His resources as our spiritual GPS system. All we have to do is ask for His guidance. God comes into our lives and works in our lives through invitation. We need to remember God has all of the latest eventualities already programmed into His plan and He desires to give us the best. Guiding is His responsibility, but He cannot guide us until we place our trust in Him. God does not force His will on us. Mankind is created with the freedom of choice or free will. As we mentioned earlier, God enters our lives through invitation! We invite God into our lives by accessing Him through prayer. When we pray to God, the simple act of praying is the divine act of acknowledging Him. Acknowledging God and inviting Him to work in our lives is the spiritual equivalent of turning on our GPS system.

Without prayer we travel down the road lost. We may have the power to correct the course right beside us, but we are not plugged into the power source. We must have a willingness to be plugged into the power source and the desire to turn the GPS system on. That willingness is expressed in our attitude of submission and obedience to God's direction. Trust is the on switch to God's spiritual direction, prayer is the way we access it, and obedience is the way we follow it.

---

[30] C. S. Lewis, *The Great Divorce* (New York: Touchstone Publishing, Simon & Schuster Inc., 1946), 9–10.

One of the most amazing things about God's spiritual GPS system is we have the ability to access it at anytime or anyplace simply by asking. No matter what stage of the journey we are on, we can stop, make a correction, and get on the right path.

Should I Ignore My Own Interests?

There exists a tension sometimes between living a life of faith and following our own personal pursuits. Occasionally we will come face to face with this dilemma: "Does this mean that I should not pray for my own interests?" The truth is God expects us to pray for ourselves, our interests, and for other things that affect our lives. There is nothing wrong with praying for specific needs and outcomes. In fact, the Bible instructs us to in James 5:16: "Confess your faults one to another, and pray one for another, that you might be healed. The effective fervent prayer of a righteous man availeth much." We are encouraged to pray for specific outcomes, and we are directed to intercede for one another. God has equipped us with an extraordinary human computer known as the *brain*. He has placed throughout our entire body emotional stimuli and impulses that feed information to the brain about the environment around us. We are directly and indirectly affected by each our five senses—hearing, touching, smelling, seeing, and tasting. Each one of these senses brings a higher quality of life to us.

Even Jesus prayed specifically for personal outcomes in life, and while doing so, He set the perfect example of how we ought to pray. On the night of His betrayal, Jesus went to the Garden of Gethsemane to pray for His life to be extended. Many scholars believe that Jesus did not feel, from His human perspective, that the disciples were ready to take over the earthly ministry for the Kingdom of God. It is possible He felt they needed more preparation, more training, and more hands-on direction. This may have led Him to pray that His life be spared or extended for a time. "O Father, if it be possible, let

THE TWO THINGS THAT MATTER MOST

this cup pass from me."[31] This request was a personal and specific prayer by the Son of God. Jesus was looking for a specific outcome from God the Father, and He hoped and prayed that God would hear and answer His request.

But God—who is all-knowing and all-powerful—had a different outcome in mind. God's plan extended beyond the disciples and the immediate circumstances that surrounded their ministries. The Father's plan included a plan for total redemption, including every single human being that has ever lived. You and I, as believers, were to be the beneficiaries of His plan. God also knew in advance what the power of the Resurrection would do in the lives of the disciples. Christ had been exposed to their humanness and shortcomings on earth. He was aware of their tendencies to be zealous and self-righteous. He knew of their fearfulness and inclination to run and hide in the face of conflict. At the time He prayed, Christ had not yet experienced the transforming power of the resurrection, but God knew. God recognized all of the factors involved in the life and death of Jesus, and the Father had available all the resources necessary to effect the best possible outcome. God is omniscient, omnipotent, and omnipresent, all of which enable Him to bring good out of any circumstances.

The Right Perspective

Jesus gives us a model for specific prayer. In every case where Jesus sought a specific outcome from God, He always prayed for God's will to be done. It was God's will that reigned supreme, it was God's will that had veto rights over everything He did, and it was God's will He ultimately sought. Jesus prayed with this important caveat: *"Not My will, but Yours be done."* When Christ prayed in this manner, it modeled dependency on God and demonstrated a trust

---

[31]   Matthew 26:39–42, Mark 14:35–36, Luke 22:41–42.

in God that He knew would lead to the best outcome. This prayer illustrates the trust that we are to have in God as well. It is a little act of submission on our part, but it unleashes the power of God in our lives so that His greater good is accomplished in us and through us.

The Apostle Paul provides one of over three thousand promises in the Bible, critical to our understanding, of how powerful this trust is in our lives. We find it in Romans 8:28: "And we know that all things work together for good to them that love God, to them who are the called according to His purposes."[32] This is a promise that ensures that whatever circumstance we find ourselves in, God will work out all of the details and will work through all obstacles to bring about the best results for ourgreatest good. Pastor and author Robert Morgan, in his book *The Promise*, states it this way, "In Christ, we have an ironclad, unfailing, all-encompassing, God-given guarantee that every single circumstance in life will sooner or later turn out well for those committed to Him."[33] Since God already knows the outcome of the events that affect our lives and seeks our greatest good, it seems reasonable that we would give Him veto rights over every choice we make.

[32] Romans 8:28 (KJV); Scofield Study Bible. (New York, NY. Oxford University Press. 1998). 1430.

[33] Robert J. Morgan, preface to *The Promise* (Nashville: B & H Publishing Group, 2008), xviii.

CHAPTER FOUR

Seeking God's Best

A Good Goal in Life

I think it is wonderful when people know at a young age what they would like to do with their lives. It helps direct their educational pursuits, and it fuels their interest and provides motivation for what they would like to accomplish. For instance, consider the life of Anne Frank of Amsterdam. Although her life was short, she made a large impact on those around her and even on our culture today. She stands as a shining example of a young person who had heart and integrity and wisdom regarding the human soul even though her time on earth was brief. Anne Frank was a Jewish girl who went into hiding during World War II to avoid the Nazis. Together with seven others, she hid in the secret annex on the Prinsengracht 263 in Amsterdam. After nearly two years in hiding they were discovered and deported into concentration camps. Anne's father, Otto Frank, was the only one of the eight people to survive. Anne Frank became world famous after her death because of the diary she wrote while in hiding.

One of the things Anne writes about is the human potential each person possesses. She writes, "Everyone has inside of him a piece of good news. The good news is that you don't know how great you can be! How much you can love! What you can accomplish! And what your potential is!"[34] What a wonderful perspective on life and its possibilities. In a way, Anne is describing the spiritual DNA that is deposited into our lives as we are created by God. Anne Frank was only fifteen years old when she died of typhus in the Bergen-Belsen concentration camp in March of 1945.[35] She left behind a youthful insight into the understanding of the human spirit and the way God uses our hearts and minds to reveal the uniqueness He created in us. She wrote eloquently about having a natural desire to know and fulfill life's purposes.

Why Am I Here?

Pastor Rick Warren, of Saddleback Community Church, tapped into that idea a number of years ago when he wrote the best-selling book *The Purpose Driven Life*. The overriding theme of the book was "life is a gift from God" and God creates everything with purpose. Life is no accident or series of haphazard coincidences. Life happens intentionally and with purpose! Furthermore, each person has his or her own unique, specially designed, individual purpose to fulfill, like pieces of a puzzle. Each piece of the humanity puzzle helps complete the picture of God's creation. Each piece represents a life, and each life is important. No particular life is any more important than another because each piece is necessary to complete the puzzle. Our primary goal in life should be to discover how we fit into the humanity puzzle. The amazing thing about a puzzle is that the pieces

---

[34]   Anne Frank, *The Diary of a Young Girl* (New York: Bantam, 1993).
[35]   "Anne Frank Biography," "Biography," accessed July 11, 2014, http://biography.org/people/anne-frank.

are shaped and colored differently, so only one piece fits perfectly in place.

Our lives are shaped in such a way as to fit perfectly into place in families, communities, work environments, and even social settings. If we live a balanced, godly life with the right perspective of seeking God's will, there is no way for us to fail. But if we try to force ourselves into situations not designed for us, the pieces of our life will not fit properly. The result is cheating ourselves of seeing the best in life, the complete picture of what God intended for us. We don't experience His best in life because we are missing the fullness of life.

We already know two important things concerning life. First, we know we are created. No one gets here on earth by willing themselves into being. We are born into existence by the actions and the will of other people apart from ourselves. Secondly, we know intelligent life, a Master Designer, God, creates with purpose. Each one of us is different. No two people completely alike. Even identical twins have different fingerprints. Therefore, we see the importance of special design and seeing ourselves as one-of-a-kind people. The Bible clearly states we are "fearfully and wonderfully made," and it attributes that wonderful work to God.[36]

If we consider several other verses in the Old Testament—for example, the Book of Jeremiah-- we see that we are made by God in accordance with a specific plan for life. "For I know the thoughts that I think toward you, says the LORD, thoughts of peace and not of evil, to give you a future and a hope. Then you will call upon Me and go and pray to Me, and I will listen to you. And you will seek Me and find [Me], when you search for Me with all your heart." [37] God is not as distant as many people make Him out to be. In the Book of Jeremiah God acknowledges He knows the thoughts and plans He

---

[36]   Psalm 139:14
[37]   Jeremiah 29:11–13 (NKJV).

has for us. His plan consists of giving us hope and a future. Isn't that what we are seeking?

In the pursuit of finding our purpose and achieving our goals in life, God asks us to do one thing, call out to Him and pray. God says the first step in finding our purpose is communicating with Him. There is no way to find the answers without first asking the question. Therefore, God encourages us to talk with Him, communicate with Him, and our questions will be answered. We are given a promise from God that He will listen to us and provide answers for us based on our personal relationship with Him. Isn't this one of the greatest things we can do?

Where Do I Go from Here?

The human heart must have a willingness to "follow"! Following requires obedience, and obedience comes through faith. Our faith will lead us toward decisions of commitment. To follow is defined as "to go or to come after, to proceed along, or to engage in as a way of life."[38] For the purposes of our understanding, our simple definition of *following* will be "to engage in as a way of life." When Jesus began His ministry, He was walking by the Sea of Galilee, and He told Peter and Andrew to "follow Him and He would make them fishers of men." They immediately left their nets and followed. When Jesus saw James and his brother John a short time later, He called out to them, and the Bible says, "They left their boat and their father, and followed Him." The pattern was the same with all four men, and the rest of the disciples would follow as well.

Jesus began teaching, preaching, and healing throughout the area, and we are told great multitudes began to follow Him and engage with Him *as a way of life*. To follow Christ, based on His command to "follow Him," requires obedience. Obedience is the willing-

---

[38]   *Merriam-Webster's Dictionary*, s.v. "follow."

ness to be under the authority of another and to follow the other's cause or commitment. When we develop faith in another person's ability to lead, we are more likely to commit ourselves to that person's purpose. Obviously the disciples felt they were following by faith in obedience to Christ because each one made a strong commitment to follow Christ throughout His earthly ministry.

It was only Judas Iscariot that wavered in obedience in the eleventh hour. The Bible makes a strong statement regarding his fate: "Woe to that man by whom the Son of Man is betrayed! It would have been good for that man if he had not been born." Obedience comes with a healthy price paid through our commitment and investment of resources. But lack of obedience also carries unintended consequences. We see it in the life of Judas Iscariot, a man who took his own life because of the remorse he experienced over his lack of obedience to the call God had placed on his life. Jesus asked His followers to make a commitment and "follow Him"! He taught many important lessons throughout His ministry, but none of the lessons He taught were greater than His teaching on the greatest commandment.

CHAPTER FIVE

The Destination: The Greatest Commandment

Being the Greatest

Many people have desired to be great at something—the greatest doctor, the greatest lawyer, the greatest teacher, the greatest actor. While being the greatest in some area of life is a worthwhile pursuit, there can be only one "greatest." The famous heavyweight boxing champion Muhammad Ali often referred to himself as the greatest boxing champ of all time. While he was a great boxing champion in the prime years of his boxing career, everyone does not agree that he was the greatest of all time.

A story attributed to Muhammad Ali concerns a flight he was taking and his claim to be Superman, the comic-strip hero. After the command to fasten the seatbelts was given, the airline attendant was checking all the passengers and reminded Ali to fasten his seat belt.

"Superman don't need no seat belt," replied Ali. "Superman don't need no airplane either," retorted the attendant.[39]

There can be only one person to occupy the position as "greatest." Only one feat can qualify as the "greatest feat." And only one command can be regarded as the "greatest commandment." Whatever is "greatest" is certainly worthy of our attention and our recognition.

A story is told of evangelist Billy Graham on the subject of greatness. Graeme Keith, treasurer of the Billy Graham Association and Billy's lifelong friend, says:

> I was on an elevator with Billy when another man in the elevator recognized him. He said, "You're Billy Graham, aren't you?"
>
> "Yes," Billy said.
>
> "Well," the man said, "you are truly a great man."
>
> Billy immediately responded, "No, I'm not a great man. I just have a great message."[40]

Few would argue with Graham's point. Dr. Graham is easily considered one of the greatest evangelists the world has known. He spent his life following Christ. He communicated, arguably, the greatest message ever communicated to mankind. It was located in the Gospel Book of John and came directly from the heart of God: "For God so loved the world that He gave His only begotten Son, that whoever believes in Him should not perish but have everlast-

---

[39]   "Back Ali," Snopes, accessed May 15, 2015, http://www.snopes.com/quotes/ali.asp.

[40]   Harold Myra and Marshall Shelley, *The Leadership Secrets of Billy Graham* (Grand Rapids: Zondervan, 2005).

ing life."[41] Dr. Harold Willmington, of Liberty University, once said John 3:16 contains nine of the most profound truths ever recorded:

1. "For God"—The greatest Person
2. "So loved the world"—The greatest truth
3. "That he gave"—The greatest act
4. "His only begotten Son"—The greatest gift
5. "That whosoever"—The greatest number of people
6. "Believeth in Him"—The greatest invitation
7. "Should not perish"—The greatest promise
8. "But have"—The greatest certainty
9. "Everlasting life"—The greatest destiny.[42]

Along with John 3:16, the greatest hope Jesus Christ gave us is the Greatest Commandment. We find it recorded in the Gospel of Matthew and the Gospel of Mark. For our purposes, we will consider the account found in the Gospel of Mark 12:28–34. When we think of the term *greatest,* we imagine the pinnacle of excellence or distinction.

The Greatest Teaching of Jesus

> Then one of the scribes came, and having heard them reasoning together, perceiving that He had answered them well, asked Him, "Which is the first commandment of all?"
>
> Jesus answered him, "The first of all the commandments is: 'Hear, O Israel, the LORD our God,

---

[41]   John 3:16 (NKJV).

[42]   Harold Willmington, "What You Need to Know about Thanksgiving," Home Bible Institute Program 2012, Liberty University.

the Lord is one. And you shall love the Lord your God with all your heart, with all your soul, with all your mind, and with all your strength.' This is the first commandment."

And the second, like it, is this: 'You shall love your neighbor as yourself.' There is no other commandment greater than these."

So the scribe said to Him, "Well said, Teacher. You have spoken the truth, for there is one God, and there is no other but He. And to love Him with all the heart, with all the understanding, with all the soul, and with all the strength, and to love one's neighbor as one-self, is more than all the whole burnt offerings and sacrifices."

Now when Jesus saw that he answered wisely, He said to him, "You are not far from the kingdom of God."

But after that no one dared question Him."
(Mark 12:28–34, NKJV)

Jesus was approached on one occasion by one of the teachers of the law, an educated person (a scribe, perhaps a Pharisee), who had been listening to His response to the Sadducees concerning the resurrection. The young teacher, apparently impressed with Jesus's response, asked Him, "Which is the first commandment of all?" This could have demonstrated an interest in seeing how Christ prioritized the things of life. Or it could have represented an opportunity to test Jesus's priority and hold His teaching under a higher level of scrutiny. We do know the young teacher or scribe would have been referencing the total number of commands, the 613 commandments out of Jewish Law. There were 248 positive commands and 365 prohibitions for the Jewish people.[43]

This young teacher wanted to know which one was first, which one was most important, which one had the preeminence, and which one had the distinction of being the greatest pursuit in life. The question itself suggests a prioritization of the events and activities in our lives to achieve life's best. When Jesus responded, he not only answered the question, He summarized the entire law by citing the two most important pursuits in life. The young man may have been a little shocked to find out life could be reduced to only two important things. Jesus told him that life is really about having two primary pursuits. If the man wanted to be successful, these pursuits were not optional; they were not suggestions or recommendations. These two things would be required.

Jesus Gives the First Commandment

Jesus said, "Hear, O Israel, the LORD our God, the LORD is one. And you shall love the LORD your God with all your heart, with all your soul, with all your mind, and with all your strength. This is the first commandment." Jesus began with the opening words of the *Shema* (a daily confessional of Israel repeated twice a day, morning and evening, by devout Jews).[44] "Oh, hear Israel, the Lord [Yahweh] our God, the Lord is one." This was designed to get the attention of everyone within the sound of Jesus's voice and not just the one asking the question. The purpose was so everyone could hear, everyone could understand, and everyone who was willing could be taught. Jesus said the greatest commandment, the one thing that rises above

---

[43] David E. Garland, *The NIV Application Commentary: Mark* (Grand Rapids: Zondervan, 1996), 476.

[44] John Walvoord and Roy Zuck, *The Bible Knowledge Commentary* (Victor Books, 1983), 164.

anything you can do, is "to love the Lord your God with all your heart, with all your soul, with all your mind and with all your strength."

Notice that Jesus did not say "you are to love My God with all your heart." He said, "You are to love *your* God with all your heart." This emphasis shows a personal intimate relationship that is to be developed with God. It is impossible to love something with which we have no relationship. We can have an appreciation for something. We can have admiration for something, but we cannot truly love something without having a personal relationship with it. Jesus tells us unequivocally, we are to have a relationship with God and love Him with all of our heart, soul, mind, and strength.

Jesus Gives the Second Commandment

The second similar command is to "love your neighbor as yourself." While these concepts may seem to be lofty goals, Jesus actually makes it pretty simple. What could be necessary to comply with Jesus's admonition? How are we to accomplish these tasks? What do we need to do? Jim Cymbala in his book *Fresh Wind, Fresh Fire* tells of a longtime friend by the name of David Jeremiah, pastor of Shadow Mountain Community Church near San Diego, California, who called his ministry one day. Dr. Jeremiah had been diagnosed with cancer, and he called to request prayer. Several months later he visited the ministry and expressed his gratitude to the congregation who interceded on his behalf to God. This was his testimony: "I called here as soon as I learned of my sickness because I knew of your emphasis on prayer. In fact, someone just greeted me in the lobby and remarked, 'Pastor Jeremiah, we really cried out to God on your behalf.' That is why I called you. I know your praying wouldn't be just some mechanical exercise but a real calling out to God with passion for my need. And God brought me through the ordeal."[45] Dr. David Jeremiah's story and his relationship with Jim Cymbala and the ministry of the Brooklyn Tabernacle Church demonstrate what it means when we are to love our neighbors as ourselves. We will explore this further in just a few moments; let's first take a look at the first commandment.

[45] Jim Cymbala and Dean Merrill, *Fresh Wind, Fresh Fire* (Grand Rapids: Zondervan, 1997), 55.

CHAPTER SIX

To Love God with All Your Heart

A Total Commitment

The last chapter ended with Jesus declaring the two most important pursuits in life: To love the Lord your God with all your heart, with all your soul, with all your mind and with all your strength, and to love your neighbor as yourself." These commandments seem pretty straightforward and simple on the surface. But to understand the biblical significance of what Jesus was teaching, one must take a closer spiritual look. Let's break down the commandments in bite-size chunks so we can better digest what Jesus was telling us.

First let us examine "To love the Lord your God with all your heart." Jesus used the heart as a descriptive metaphor of total commitment. His audience would have understood what He meant. Even today we have a good understanding of what He meant because of our relationship with our own heart. The heart that beats within each of us is an amazing organ. It performs its work of pumping blood throughout the circulatory system of our body, pumping life and oxygen into each and every cell, and it does so because of the way it was created. The heart does not see, the heart does not hear, nor does it taste or touch, but it is vital to the other organs that do.

Professor David E. Garland of Louisville, Kentucky, says the heart "is the command center of the body, where decisions are made and plans are hatched. It is the center of our inner being, which controls our feelings, emotions, desires, and passions."[46] Without the heart there would be no life, no feeling, no passion, no desire, or any other physical function. The heart is critical to our existence, and the heart is at work twenty-four hours a day, seven days a week providing life. The heart does not have to be told to beat every couple of seconds. It beats automatically and systematically to insure internal stability between other members of our bodies. The heart has been created and designed for a total commitment to life.

Having a meaningful life without the function of the heart simply is not possible. This writer believes this is the single most important reason Jesus singles out the heart as the first and primary motivation regarding the love we are to have for God. We are motivated in life by the passions of our hearts. We excel in activities we are most keenly interested in because of its function. We research; we investigate and accumulate information linking our interests to our pursuit of the important activities of our lives because they become our heart's desire. They are the things that make life meaningful. They become the things we are passionate about!

What Passion Looks Like

Let me share an example of the type of passion we are speaking about. It is found in the life of Kathy Holmgren, wife of Mike Holmgren, former NFL coach of the Seattle Seahawks, whose team

---

[46]   David E. Garland, *The NIV Application Commentary: Mark* (Grand Rapids: Zondervan, 1996), 481.

---

oxygen into each and every cell, and it does so because of the way it was created. The heart does not see, the heart does not hear, nor does it taste or touch, but it is vital to the other organs that do.

Professor David E. Garland of Louisville, Kentucky, says the heart "is the command center of the body, where decisions are made and plans are hatched. It is the center of our inner being, which controls our feelings, emotions, desires, and passions."[46] Without the heart there would be no life, no feeling, no passion, no desire, or any other physical function. The heart is critical to our existence, and the heart is at work twenty-four hours a day, seven days a week providing life. The heart does not have to be told to beat every couple of seconds. It beats automatically and systematically to insure internal stability between other members of our bodies. The heart has been created and designed for a total commitment to life.

Having a meaningful life without the function of the heart simply is not possible. This writer believes this is the single most important reason Jesus singles out the heart as the first and primary motivation regarding the love we are to have for God. We are motivated in life by the passions of our hearts. We excel in activities we are most keenly interested in because of its function. We research; we investigate and accumulate information linking our interests to our pursuit of the important activities of our lives because they become our heart's desire. They are the things that make life meaningful. They become the things we are passionate about!

What Passion Looks Like

Let me share an example of the type of passion we are speaking about. It is found in the life of Kathy Holmgren, wife of Mike Holmgren, former NFL coach of the Seattle Seahawks, whose team

---

[46]   David E. Garland, *The NIV Application Commentary: Mark* (Grand Rapids: Zondervan, 1996), 481.

found itself playing in the Super Bowl. The Super Bowl is one of the most anticipated events in America each year. With the championship of the NFL on the line, entertaining commercials, and a spectacular halftime show, an estimated 190 million people watched the game in 2006. And one would assume the wife of one of the head coaches in the game would be one of those 190 million. But Kathy Holmgren decided to skip Super Bowl XL, and Detroit, for something she considered more important—a faith-based humanitarian trip to Africa.

Kathy Holmgren and her daughter, Calla, left three days before the big game on a seventeen-day medical training mission with Northwest Medical Teams—a relief group based in Portland, Oregon—to the northwest region of the Democratic Republic of Congo. A nurse and obstetrician, respectively, the two joined six other physicians with experience as missionaries.

During the three days it took to reach the region, the medical team traveled over marginal roads that narrowed to near nonexistence, waded through streams, and crossed rough-hewn and often improvised bridges. While much of the world tuned in to the Super Bowl, the team was working with the staff of a hospital operated by the Evangelical Covenant Church, the denomination the Holmgrens belong to. The hospital is the only medical facility for 300,000 people in the region, and the staff is often forced to use rudimentary equipment when treating 2,500 patients a month. More than 3.9 million Congolese have died since 1998, most from preventable diseases, according to the British medical journal *The Lancet.*

Kathy Holmgren spent ten months in the region during 1970 but gave up her dream of being a Covenant medical missionary to marry. The previous October, Mike Holmgren's birthday present to his wife was the trip back to the country she loves. The family did not consider the two women might miss the Super Bowl. "I don't think we paid much attention to the date," Kathy said. "As the possibility of our being in the game became a reality, we decided to continue with our plans. The actual game makes me so nervous, so I don't watch anyway, and we feel like this trip is important."[47] The fact that Kathy Holmgren would avoid the distractions and all of the fanfare leading up to one of the most anticipated events of the year in order to pursue a mission of service reveals a deep passion and love she held in her heart for other people.

Our hearts will always pursue the things that we prioritize as most important to us. There will be constant things in life to pull us in different directions, but we are the ones who prioritize. We are the ones who put things in order. We may have different priorities, different crises, different challenges, and different distractions, but what remain constant are the things we are passionate about; those things always become our heart's desire. The things we have etched in our heart, the things that we are totally committed to are the things we will pursue. When things in life distract us and take us away from the normal activities, the heart acts as its own GPS system bringing us back to the things we are passionate about.

That is why loving God with all our heart is so important. God is not interested in our loving Him halfheartedly. A halfhearted love wanes under the pressures and distractions of life. Halfhearted love is self-prioritizing, pushing concerns and activities to a lower level of things we would like to do. They include the types of things we feel we will get to just as soon as there is an opening in our schedule or our time is more flexible, but unfortunately they are all too often the things we never get back to. The problem with items falling into a "halfhearted-love category" is they eventually lose our attention and our attraction. They are placed on the back burner, so to speak, and

---

[47] "Coach's Wife Chooses Missions over Super Bowl," Preaching Today, accessed August 15, 2014, http://www.preachingtoday.com/illustrations/2006/march/4031306.html.

they become out of sight, out of mind. Halfhearted love cools down, and we lose our passion and drive. We want our important relationships to be the ones we cherish most, those driven with a desire for closeness, an interest in others and a concern for them.

That is exactly how God feels toward each of us. He desires a love so complete and so deep it completely consumes our heart. Our love for God should be as automatic and consistent as our heartbeat, connecting us to a daily relationship with our Creator that says, "You are the most important consideration of the day. How can I serve You?" The late Dr. Howard Hendricks of Dallas Theological Seminary once said, "Each of us needs to take into account the way that God has uniquely and individually designed us. We also need to see that our lives matter beyond our own personal concerns. God's purpose is that we become His agents of transformation for the world around us." And he goes on to say:

King Solomon had a similar vision in mind when, near the end of his life, he prayed:

O God, Thou hast taught me from my youth;
And I still declare Thy wondrous deeds.
And even when I am old and gray, O God,
do not forsake me,
Until I declare Thy strength to this generation,
Thy power to all who are to come.

Psalm 71:17–18[48]

God desires the love of our whole heart because a wholehearted love motivates us to live as He originally designed us. It gives our

---

[48] Howard Hendricks and William Hendricks, *Living By the Book* (Chicago: Moody Publishers, 2007), 11.

life's purpose and fills our lives with promise. To love with all your heart is to be totally committed to the highest possible cause. Dr. David E. Garland says, "Love is our inner commitment to God that is expressed in all our conduct and relationships."[49] In other words, love is the reason we were created, and love is the primary purpose of our existence. God, by His very nature, is love, and we are most like God when we display His personal characteristics in our own lives. To love with all our heart means to be totally committed to a relationship that is the most important relationship we will ever experience with the most important person we will ever know, God.

The importance of this relationship hinges on the eternal nature of God and on the fact we have been made in His image and in His likeness. The only way we reach our highest level of human potential is by developing and nurturing a deep and abiding love for God that seeks out His will in preference to our own. Jesus made this evident when He prayed at Gethsemane, "Abba, Father, all things all possible for You. Take this cup away from Me; nevertheless, not what I will, but what You will."[50] Loving with all our hearts requires a willingness to submit to a higher calling and a greater purpose above and beyond what we can see or what we have previously experienced. This is the type of love that Jesus refers to when He instructs us to love God with all of our heart.

---

[49]   Garland, *The NIV Application Commentary: Mark*, 476.
[50]   Mark 14:36 (NKJV).

CHAPTER SEVEN

With All Your Soul

If you and I were having a discussion and I were to ask, "What makes you tick?" you would probably understand what I am asking is what motivates you in life. What are the things you are passionate about? How would you respond? How would you sum up your expectations for life? We know there is something inside us that makes us want to get out of bed in the morning, but exactly what? I believe the deepest motivation we have for life is located in the region of our existence known as the soul. Professor David Garland indicates that the "soul" is the source of vitality in life. It is the motivating power that brings strength of will.[51] Webster's Dictionary defines *soul* as "the spiritual part of a person that is believed to give life to the body, a person's deeply felt moral and emotional nature."[52] To consider it a little more introspectively, the soul is the immaterial essence, animating principle, or actuating cause of an individual life, it is the spiritual principle

---

[51] Garland, *The NIV Application Commentary: Mark*, 484.

[52] *Merriam-Webster Online Dictionary*, s.v. "soul," accessed October 2014, http://www.merriam-webster.com/dictionary/soul.

embodied in human beings, all rational and spiritual beings, or the universe, it is essentially a person's total self.

Perhaps a better way of looking at the soul is to say the soul is the who, what, when, where and how of each one of us. The soul is more than just our personal, spiritual DNA; the soul is the entire blueprint of our individual lives. There is no activity we are associated with more, either voluntary or involuntarily, than activity involving the soul. The soul is fully engaged in every aspect of our lives, and I believe that is one of the reasons Jesus includes it as part of the Greatest Commandment. He said we are "to love the Lord your God with all your heart, with all your soul." When Jesus spoke of the soul, He was not referring to just a cerebral ascent of the mind or a type of moral consciousness of choosing right over wrong. Jesus referenced the soul as an integral, eternal part of our existence which needs to be fully functional in every aspect of our life. He was referencing not simply consciousness, but also conscientiousness as well, being thoroughly and completely plugged into life.

Motivational speaker Zig Ziglar once said, "The foundation stones for balanced success are honesty, character, integrity, faith, love, and loyalty, and each individual already has within themselves all of the qualities necessary for success."[53] The reason this statement resonates with successful people is because many of these qualities are the major ingredients that make up the soul. They are spiritual attributes related to the nature of God and distributed to each individual with the purpose of producing the very best fruit in the lives of mankind.

Sometimes we hear people referred to as "the heart and soul" of an organization, or a person may be the "face" of a particular movement. The reason people are referred to in this manner is because

---

[53] Successories, *Great Quotes from Zig Ziglar* (Franklin Lakes: Career Press, 1997), 52–53.

those individuals embody the vision, idea, or concept of an organization. The organization is fueled and energized by the total level of commitment emanating from the qualities of a particular person. When a person pours heart and soul into a body of work, they essentially give their entire self to the project. The results are usually reflective of an individual's own personal qualities, and many people will say at the completion of a project, "It captured the person's soul." The soul, therefore, is recognizable and identifiable as a reflection of who we are beyond our surface-level personality.

Our soul is very much a part of our daily existence and is often the driver of what motivates our actions. When we love God with all of our soul, it suggests moving into a deeper spiritual acknowledging of the greatness of God and the smallness of self. John the Baptist said of Jesus, "He must increase, and I must decrease. He who comes from above is above all, he who is of the earth is earthly and speaks of the earth."[54] To love God with all of our soul is to acknowledge God's greatness and say in our own spirit, "He must increase and I must decrease." It allows God to occupy His rightful place in our heart and soul and it puts our spiritual equilibrium in perspective and it allows us to meet the expectations of loving God.

A humorous article written for the magazine *Business Insider* and titled "We Calculated How Much Your Soul Is Actually Worth" tried to estimate how much a soul is worth in real dollars. The article admitted that the business of soul evaluating isn't an exact science and offered several examples. For instance, at the low end there's a comical incident where Homer Simpson sells his soul to the devil for one donut, estimated at about $1. Also included was an award-winning short story from the 1930s called "The Devil and Daniel Webster," which suggested another estimate. In the story, a man named Jabez Stone sells his soul to the devil for ten years of prosperity. *Business*

---

[54]   John 3:30–31 (NKJV).

Insider notes that had that story taken place in today's marketplace, that would have made his soul worth approximately $1,745,926. But the article concludes that perhaps the best estimate of the value of the human soul may come from the US government's Environmental Protection Agency. The EPA uses what it calls the VSL (or value of a statistical life) to determine the worth of a soul, and currently the VSL estimate is at $8.6 million.[55]

In reality though, I believe most people know the human soul is priceless. Jesus, speaking on the topic of discipleship, asked a question that highlighted the value of a human soul, "For what will it profit a man [meaning mankind] if he gains the whole world, and loses his own soul?"[56] The question implies the permanence and eternal nature of the human soul. It suggests a value greater than all of the accumulated wealth of the whole world. One solitary, individual soul carries more value than all of the material wealth added and multiplied together, which is quite impressive. Jesus can rightly make that claim because of the temporal and fleeing nature of earthly possessions. The Bible is very clear that the world and everything in it will one day pass away and will not last forever. The world is on God's timetable, and the clock is ticking.

The soul, on the other hand, is permanent and everlasting. God created the soul and placed it within the confines of our human tabernacle, which is a biblical reference to our bodies. God designed the soul so mankind could forever have a permanent relationship with God that would transcend recordable time. The soul is the supernatural ingredient designed by God and imparted to humans that link us to godlikeness. Notice what God said in the Book of Beginnings

---

[55] Walter Hickey, "We Calculated How Much Your Soul Is Actually Worth," *Business Insider,* September 30, 13, http://www.businessinsider.com/how-much-is-your-soul-worth-2013-9.

[56] Mark 8:36 (NKJV).

(Genesis): "Then God said, 'Let Us make man in Our image, according to Our likeness; let them have dominion over the fish of the sea, over the birds of the air, and over the cattle, over all the earth and over every creeping thing that creeps on the earth. So God created man in His own image; in the image He created him; male and female He created them."[57]

When Jesus said that we are to love God "with all of our heart and all of our soul," He was speaking of a total commitment of everything we experience, especially things associated with the heart. But Jesus carries it to a higher level when He mentions the soul. Jesus elevates the love we are to have for God to a supernatural level. The soul represents things of a permanent nature with God, things that are eternal. The type of love Jesus refers to "with all our heart and all our soul" is a love that exceeds our human (temporal) nature and incorporates our supernatural (eternal) nature—namely, the soul. Let's explore a little further!

---

[57] Genesis 1:26–27 (NKJV).

CHAPTER EIGHT

With All Your Mind

The Human "On-Star"

A number of years ago I took a trip to Israel, and I shared a room with a young man who was vice president of a local Bank. He and I became good friends in a short period of time since both of us were experiencing graduate school well into our vocational careers. I was employed by the Postal Service as one of their managers, and I served a small congregation as a bivocational pastor. Our trip to Israel left an indelible mark on both of our lives. Shortly after returning home and resuming our responsibilities, my banking friend informed me that he felt a calling to become a missionary. In a discussion that we had, he told me he was considering resigning his position as vice president and city executive with the local bank and entering into ministry as a missionary. At the time, he had three young children, his wife home-schooled, and he was the primary financial support for the family. So my obvious reaction to this new revelation was "Have you lost your mind?" It just did not seem reasonable, practical, or even financially feasible to think God would call someone to make such an impractical decision. After all, I know God, and I know God does not ask reasonable people to do stupid stuff! Right?

Occasionally there may be situations that seem to defy the laws of logic and reason, but they are the exception, rather than the rule I reasoned!

Our brain is uniquely designed by God to calculate, evaluate, and determine the best possible options for our decision-making process. Dr. David Garland of Southern Baptist Seminary tells us "the 'mind' is the faculty of perception and reflection that directs our opinions and judgments."[58] We rely on the power of reason, contemplation, and thought to guide our lives. We make hundreds of decisions each day without giving much thought to how much we are relying on the brain to guide us through the process. It is not that we take the brain for granted; we simply use it so much it is impossible to function effectively without it. In fact, when we are mentally drained after a day of intellectual calisthenics, we refer to ourselves as being "brain dead." Our mind becomes exhausted, and we find ourselves in need of a temporary reprieve, a break from mental activity. The brain is so crucial to our existence many people have undertaken studies to unlock its mysteries and to better understand its processes.

In an article titled, *Brain's Complexity is Beyond Anything Imagined,* author and Science Writer Brian Thomas, M.S., writes, "The brain has for a long time been compared to man-made computers in its astounding ability to process, store and route information. Stanford University professor and senior study author Stephen Smith said that "one synapse may contain on the order of 1,000 molecular-scale switches. A single human brain has more switches than all the computers and routers and Internet connections on Earth." Thomas goes on to say, "The more complicated a system is, the stronger it argues for having been intentionally designed. And

---

[58]   David E. Garland, *The NIV Application Commentary: Mark,* 484.

brains certainly qualify, despite assertions that random-acting natural processes somehow assembled them. In these cases, the burden of proof lies heavily on those who insist that such systems are not in fact what they plainly appear to be: the products of intentional ingenious design. The God of the Bible stands as the most tenable source of the specified complexity of interconnected neurons upon which human and much animal life depends."

http://www.icr.org/article/brains-complexity-is-beyond-anything/

The conclusion is the brain is an absolutely amazing organ with multifunctional capabilities. It works with such precision performing routine tasks even while a person sleeps, regulating our heartbeat, pumping air into lungs, and directing digestive systems to convert food into energy. These tasks continue in a 24/7 cycle as we wake up and begin a new day with added responsibilities of calculating, evaluating, and determining what new things we desire to accomplish.

It is with this understanding that Jesus gave us the remarkable command, "You shall love the LORD your God with all your heart, with all your soul, with all your mind." Our brains are always functioning in some capacity. When Jesus tells us we are to love God "with all of our mind," it infers a love that is so natural and so constant it is happening all the time. It happens both consciously and unconsciously because it is instinctive rather than coercive. If, for example, we love as a result of being loved, it falls short of the standard established by Christ. A well-defined love for God needs to be as natural as the heart pumping blood or the lungs distributing oxygen. It should flow out of a heart shaped by the goodness of God's grace and a soul appreciative of God's mercy and a mind that fully understands both. We are to love God with all of our heart, our soul, and our mind.

CHAPTER NINE

With All Your Strength

How Much Strength?

Perhaps one of the most unknowable aspects of our lives is how much individual strength we possess physically, intellectually, emotionally, or even spiritually. People have a tendency either to underestimate or overestimate their own level of strength depending on their circumstances. Throughout history a few people have demonstrated some amazing feats of strength when faced with critical, life-changing situations. One such example was reported by NBC reporter Meghan Holohan, who shared the story of Lauren Kornacki. Lauren discovered her father crushed beneath his BMW 525i, which had slipped off the car jack as he was working on it. The twenty-two-year-old wedged herself under the midsized vehicle, picked up the rear of the car on the right side. The rear wheel had been removed while he worked on the car, and the car had fallen on his chest. She used her strength to lift the car off her father and pulled him out to safety. She then administered CPR on him until rescue personnel arrived and transported him the hospital. It raises the question, where did Lauren get this amazing strength? The article goes on to say:

We hear tales from time to time of people exhibiting superhuman strength in life-and-death emergencies. After experiencing amazement over such a feat, we all wonder: How can a regular person lift something that weighs more than a ton?

Actually, most people "can lift six to seven times their body weight," says Michael Regnier, professor and vice chair of bioengineering at the University of Washington. But most people don't push themselves so hard, though athletes often push themselves more than most. Fear, fatigue, and pain prevent people from attempting feats of amazing strength in daily life, says Dr. Javier Provencio, director of the neurological ICU at Cleveland Clinic.[59]

Sometimes individuals possess more strength than they are aware of because they regularly function on a level less than their strength capacity. Their argument would be "I know my limitations, and I'm staying within them." But do we really know our limitation? Do we know our strengths?

Knowing More about Ourselves

While attending seminary, this writer had to complete a course titled Growth and Development of the Contemporary Minister. The syllabus description said the course was designed to take an in-depth look at the person in ministry—namely, people who had signed up

---

[59]   Meghan Holohan, "How do people find the superhuman strength to lift cars?" *NBC News*, August 3, 2012, accessed December 12, 2014, http://www.nbcnews.com/health/body-odd/how-do-people-find-superhuman-strength-lift-cars-f92145.

for the course. The course contained extensive psychological testing designed to develop a personal profile for each individual student. The objective was to identify strengths and weaknesses of each person and match them with measureable outcomes. The thought behind the course was by identifying weaknesses and strengths, a person could then work to improve on a particular area of life or ministry. As it turned out, this course ended up being one of the best courses in seminary for personal growth.

Knowing as much as you can about yourself is important in life because it helps you understand how you fit into the humanity puzzle. God has shaped our lives in such a way that we complement the things around us and we fit uniquely into a design that He has woven into society. Everyone has both strengths and weaknesses that develop on the outer layers of personality. Strengths and weaknesses are generally categorized as being physical, emotional, intellectual, or even spiritual in nature. Each one of those categories is important because each one becomes a component for overall development. They interact to form the essence of who we are.

It should be noted that we all have our own individual weaknesses and strengths. God has created us personally and individually so that our own personal strengths and weaknesses become the special ingredient to our own uniqueness. Simply because someone may be stronger in one area than you are or they may have a higher proficiency level at some tasks than you do, it only represents a strength they have related to that particular area. It is good to recognize our differences, both in strengths and weaknesses, because through recognition comes greater opportunities for working together.

Even the Disciples Had Issues

An interesting observation regarding the people who were closest to Jesus, particularly His half brothers James and Jude, is they lacked faith. They had trouble believing that Jesus was the Christ.

The Bible highlights an interesting conversation in the Book of John between Jesus and His brothers related to faith-based issues. We are told, "His brothers therefore said to Him, 'Depart from here and go into Judea, that Your disciples also may see the works that You are doing. For no one does anything in secret while he himself seeks to be known openly. If You do these things, show Yourself to the world.' *For even His brothers did not believe in Him.*"[60] Did you get that? Even His brothers did not believe in Him!

The brothers had witnessed the miracles, seen Him walk on water, feed the five thousand, heal a lame man in Jerusalem and a nobleman's son, but they were still skeptical of His identity. They knew He was doing some amazing things, unexplainable things, but they simply could not pull the trigger on belief. They knew there were some special qualities about Him and His ability to lead and inspire. But their inner weakness (doubt) built a wall around their hearts and minds that prevented their faith from penetrating it. The end result of their weakness made commitment difficult. John MacArthur sheds light on the weaknesses of the disciples: "All their shortcomings and human failings seemed to overshadow their potential....They lacked spiritual understanding...They lacked humility....They lacked faith....They lacked commitment....They lacked power." Why would Jesus pick twelve people who held such little potential for success? MacArthur says the answer is pretty simple: His strength (meaning the strength of God) is made perfect in (our) weakness (2 Corinthians 12:9).[61]

It was not until after the resurrection that each one of the disciples became totally sold on Christ, and their weaknesses were made strong. All the disciples became so strong and committed to Christ

60   John 7:3–5, NKJV.
61   John MacArthur, *Twelve Ordinary Men* (Nashville: W Publishing Group, 2002), 24–26.

they were willing to die martyrs' deaths with the exception of John the Apostle. John was exiled to the Isle of Patmos and lived in a cave as part of his punishment for his witness for Christ. This place would certainly have been a difficult environment for someone of John's advanced age.

To help us understand the extent of the strength developed by the disciples, author Grant R. Jeffery offers the following summation of their fates. "Most of our information about the deaths of the apostles is derived from early church traditions. While tradition is unreliable as to small details, it very seldom contains outright inventions." The following information comes from Eusebius one of the most important of the early church historians:

Matthew suffered martyrdom in Ethiopia, killed by a sword wound.

Mark died in Alexandria, Egypt, after being dragged by horses through the streets until he was dead.

Luke was hanged in Greece as a result of his tremendous preaching to the lost.

John faced martyrdom when he was boiled in a huge basin of boiling oil during a wave of persecution in Rome. However, he was miraculously delivered from death and John was then sentenced to the mines on the prison island of Patmos and lived in a cave.

Peter was crucified upside down on an x-shaped cross, according to church tradition because he told his tormentors that he felt unworthy to die in the same way that Jesus Christ had died.

James the Just, the leader of the church in Jerusalem, was thrown from the southeast pinnacle of the Temple, over a hundred feet down, when he refused to deny his faith in

Christ. When they discovered that he survived the fall, his enemies beat James to death with a fuller's club.

James the Greater, a son of Zebedee, was a fisherman by trade when Jesus called him to a lifetime of ministry. As a strong leader of the church, James was ultimately beheaded at Jerusalem. The Roman officer who guarded James watched amazed as James defended his faith at his trial. Later, the officer walked beside James to the place of execution. Overcome by conviction, he declared his new faith to the judge and knelt beside James to accept beheading as a Christian as well.

Bartholomew, also known as Nathanael, became a missionary to Asia. He witnessed of Jesus Christ in what is present day Turkey. Bartholomew was martyred for his preaching in Armenia and was believed to have been flayed to death by a whip. He may have also been crucified.

Andrew was crucified on an x-shaped cross in Patras, Greece. After being whipped severely by seven soldiers they tied his body to the cross with cords to prolong his agony. His followers reported that, when he was led toward the cross, Andrew saluted it in these words: "I have long desired and expected this happy hour. The cross has been consecrated by the body of Christ hanging on it." He continued to preach to his tormentors for two days until he expired.

Thomas was stabbed with a spear in India during one of his missionary trips to establish the church in the subcontinent.

Jude, the brother of Jesus, was killed with arrows when he refused to deny his faith in Christ.

Matthias, Matthias was chosen by the Apostles to replace Judas Iscariot, after the death of Judas in the Field of Blood. Information concerning the life and death of Matthias is vague and contradictory. One tradition maintains that Matthias was stoned at Jerusalem by the Jews, and then beheaded.

Barnabas, one of the group of seventy disciples, wrote the Epistle of Barnabas. He preached throughout Italy and Cyprus. Barnabas was stoned to death at Salonica.

Phillip was crucified, according to the plaque in the church of the Holy Apostles.

Paul was believed to have been tortured and then beheaded by the evil Emperor Nero at Rome in A.D. 67. Paul endured a lengthy imprisonment which allowed him to write his many epistles to the churches he had formed throughout the Roman Empire. These letters, which taught many of the foundational doctrines of Christianity, form a large portion of the New Testament. Church tradition says that Nero executed Paul in Rome c. 67 A.D.

Details of the martyrdoms of the disciples and apostles are found in traditional early church sources. These traditions were recounted in the writings of the church fathers and the first official church historian, Eusebius. Although we cannot at this time verify every detail historically, the universal belief of the early Christian writers was that all of the apostles had faced martyrdom faithfully without denying their faith in the resurrection of Jesus Christ.[62]

The martyrdom of those closest to Jesus in the wake of Jesus's own crucifixion provides strong evidence of their faith in Jesus and His claim to be the Messiah. It's important to note that while some of these men struggled with weakness and faith during the course of their lives, they also experienced a commitment to Christ that transformed them. I have known people who were willing to die for

---

[62] Grant R. Jeffery, "The Martyrdom of the Apostles," *Bible Probe*, accessed July 24, 2014, http://www.bibleprobe.com/apostles.htm.

a truth or a principle they believed in, but I am not aware of anyone willing to die for something they knew to be untrue or false. The disciples and the apostles demonstrated a love for God that was high-lighted by giving all they had to give for Him.

CHAPTER TEN

The Second Greatest Commandment: Love Your Neighbor as Yourself

Who Is Our Neighbor?

There is an interesting story that Jesus shares in the Book of Luke known as the story of the Good Samaritan. In the story Jesus explains the concept of neighbor based on the teaching of the Bible. We tend to think of a neighbor as one who lives next door or one who lives in the subdivision near our homes. While this would certainly be a fairly accurate description of a neighbor-neighbor, it falls short of the definition of a neighbor from a biblical standpoint.

Sometime ago I received a call from a prominent man in the local community where I lived. He called and said, "Pastor, I have a question for you concerning the Bible," so I said, "I'll be glad to help if I can." He said, "In the story of the Good Samaritan, who was the neighbor that Jesus was talking about, and what was Jesus's purpose for giving us this story?" As I spoke to him about the story and explained the spiritual significance I believe Jesus was communicating by giving us this story, the man confided that he had prejudices toward certain segments of the population he was struggling with. I would expect that if you and I were honest, most of us would find ourselves in that same category. All of us have had experiences that shape our way of thinking and provide for us a way of looking at the world.

This perspective is what we call our worldview, and we have to acknowledge that sometimes our worldview can be distorted if it is based only on our own biased experiences. The Word of God will always challenge our thinking and our motivation. But the primary purpose of the Bible is to bring us in line with God's will. When we read the Word of God, we must respond with more than an intellectual assent to greater knowledge. We must read with the expectation of applying God's Word to our lives and allowing it to change us, if necessary, to conform to God's purposes. God's Word is not simply to inform, but to transform. It is designed to transform our thinking and our actions into the image of Christ-likeness.

Understanding the Command to "Love Your Neighbor"

In Luke's Gospel a young educated lawyer comes to Jesus asking a question, "What shall I do to inherit eternal life?" That question led to the story of the Good Samaritan. The Bible says the lawyer was testing Jesus in hopes of validating his own life before Christ. Jesus had been gaining popularity as a good teacher throughout the countryside surrounding Jerusalem. Many people were coming to hear what this new teacher had to say about life. His teaching was unlike the teaching of many of His contemporaries, and many questions were being raised. This young lawyer, out of curiosity, confusion, or ignorance, made an inquiry that led to the story of the Good Samaritan.

It should be understood, the Christian faith will always accommodate sincere questions because the Christian faith is built on a foundation of truth. Truth and Christianity do not compete, but complement each other. This story begins: "And behold, a certain lawyer stood up and tested Him, saying, 'Teacher, what shall I do to inherit eternal life?'"[63] Again this is perhaps the most important question that anyone will ever ask in life. This young lawyer sought to reassure himself that he was doing the right thing, so he made an inquiry of Jesus. Jesus used this as a teaching moment and began to tell him a story that highlighted what was needed in order to inherit eternal life. What becomes interesting is Jesus extends His answer to include our personal responsibilities to our "neighbors" as well.

He points out a spiritual truth and raises the questions "What is written in the Law?" and "How do you interpret it?"

> So he answered and said, "You shall love the LORD your God with all your heart, with all your soul, with all your strength, and with all your mind, and your neighbor as yourself."
>
> And He said to him, "You have answered rightly; do this and you will live."[64]

Jesus commends the answer by saying "you're right, do it and live." Nothing fancy, no big spiritual commentary, no flowery words, no additional requirements to contribute to charitable organizations or serve on Church committees. In fact, the surprising thing is there was nothing new in what Jesus was sharing in His response. It was a fundamental ethical call *to love God and to respond to others in light of that love.* This was the type of conduct and behavior expected

---

[63] Luke 10:25 (NKJV).
[64] Luke 10:27–28 (NKJV).

of everyone, and it probably surprised Jesus that the young lawyer seemed so ignorant of the requirements. Jesus again distills life down two simple tasks:

- Love, God with all your heart, soul, mind, and strength.
- And love others like you love yourself.

I used the word *simple* in describing these two tasks, but you and I know it is anything but simple in its application. If you love God with all your heart, soul, mind, and strength, it will require a commitment of everything you have. It will cause people to prioritize God's will over their own self-will. It will force us to make choices and sacrifices. We are used to making choices, but we don't like to make "sacrifices." Sacrifices make us eliminate things from our lives that we have grown attached to. If we were to be completely honest with ourselves, sacrifices separate the nominal Christians from the committed ones. If we were transparent, most of us really only love God with a part of our heart (halfheartedly), part of our mind, a part of our soul, and with minimum strength! Even on the best days we have trouble reaching God's basic standard.

But when we consider the second part of the admonition from Christ, "love your neighbor as yourself," it almost sounds impossible. On this particular command, we don't even come close. The young lawyer in the story challenges Jesus on the issue of "Who is my neighbor?" This is where the story really gets good because Jesus is about to turn his world upside down.

Who Is My Neighbor?

Professor Darrell Bock of Dallas Theological Seminary says, "Jesus' capacity for turning an abstract theological discussion into a story of real-life issues is amazing. The story of the 'Good Samaritan' reveals how God refuses to allow distinctions to be made when it comes to the treatment of people."[65] It should be noted: *The scribes and Pharisees viewed only the righteous as being a neighbor.* They taught that the wicked—including sinners, Gentiles, and especially Samaritans—were to be hated because they were the enemies of God. In their communal system of the day, they were under no obligation to respond to anyone who was not their neighbor. The suggestion that some people are "non-neighbors" is what Jesus is responding to in this story.

The story begins the way a lot of stories begin. "A man was going down from Jerusalem to Jericho" (Luke 10:30). At this point, we aren't told anything about the man. Not his nationality or even his name. He was simply a man traveling down the road. The road the man was traveling on remains, to this day, as one of the most dangerous roads in the world. The road from Jerusalem to Jericho is a little less than seventeen miles, but the road drops three thousand feet in elevation, making it very dangerous to travel especially at night.[66] The road during the time of Jesus would certainly have been a haven for thieves and robbers.

The story of the Good Samaritan:

> But he [certain lawyer], wanting to justify himself, said to Jesus, "And who is my neighbor?"
>
> Then Jesus answered and said: "A certain [man] went down from Jerusalem to Jericho, and fell among thieves, who stripped him of his clothing, wounded [him], and departed, leaving [him] half dead. Now by chance a certain priest

---

[65] Darrell L. Bock, *The NIV Application Commentary: Luke* (Grand Rapids: Zondervan Books, 1996), 299.

[66] John Walvoord and Roy Zuck, *The Bible Knowledge Commentary* (Wheaton: Victor Books, 1983), 234

came down that road. And when he saw him, he passed by on the other side. Likewise a Levite, when he arrived at the place, came and looked, and passed by on the other side. But a certain Samaritan, as he journeyed, came where he was. And when he saw him, he had compassion. So he went to [him] and bandaged his wounds, pouring on oil and wine; and he set him on his own animal, brought him to an inn, and took care of him. On the next day, when he departed, he took out two denarii, gave [them] to the innkeeper, and said to him, 'Take care of him; and whatever more you spend, when I come again, I will repay you.' "So which of these three do you think was neighbor to him who fell among the thieves?"

And he said, "He who showed mercy on him."

Then Jesus said to him, "Go and do likewise."[67]

From our story we see the man is attacked, robbed, beaten, and left half dead. There is a cultural crisis involved in this story as well as ethical issues that are raised. The priest and the Levite in the story are the ones wearing the white hats—the good guys, so to speak. They would have been the ones expected to help.

Luke 10:31: "Now by chance a certain priest came down that road. And when he saw him, he passed by on the other side."

We don't know for sure because the Bible does not provide all the details, but the man who had been robbed may have heard footsteps and thought, "Someone's coming to help me." The story suggests this particular priest may have been somewhat pious because of his actions. Maybe he thought, "I'd rather not get involved with

---

[67]   Luke 10:29–37 (NKJV).

someone else's situation. After all this isn't my problem." We can only imagine how disappointing this would have been for the man who had been robbed. To have an opportunity to be helped only to see it eliminated because other people were not interested enough to become involved. This type of situation is not unusual even in our culture. We see this same type of scene played out across our nation on a daily basis. We are not talking about over-involvement, like a busy-body, but rather concern or sensitivity toward helping others in their time of need.

In the next verse we see a similar response that is now trending in our society.

Luke 10:32: "Likewise a Levite, when he arrived at the place, came and looked and passed by on the other side."

Same situation, only this time it is a Levite, another Biblical hero. A Levite was a particular type of person who was from the priestly tribe of God's chosen people. Surely, if anyone would have compassion on another human being, it would have been our Levite. But, no, scripture states that he too passed on the other side. You wonder if the man who had been robbed began thinking, "No one cares. They just pass by, and I must have no value."

A Godly Perspective

In verse 33 we see a different attitude and a different approach to the same situation.

Luke 10:33: "But a certain Samaritan, as he journeyed, came where he was. And when he saw him, he had compassion."

Luke, the physician, reveals the answer to "Who is our neighbor?" in verse 33. The one that would not have been expected to respond, the Samaritan, becomes the neighbor. He was the outcast; he belonged to the lowest stratus of people that existed in the first century. Jesus picks the Samaritan as the hero of the story because such a person would have been a "non-neighbor" in the eyes of the lawyer and Jesus's Jewish audience.

If you look up *Samaritan* today in a modern dictionary, it says, "A person who is generous in helping those in distress."[68] The godly actions of this particular Samaritan was significant enough to have an impact on his culture and on ours today. Through his actions and his response, neighborly behavior is defined. Jesus then asked a simple question to the lawyer: "Which of the three was a neighbor to the man who fell into the hands of robbers?" Dr. Bock says, "The idea of a Good Samaritan was so conflicting for him he can't even bring himself to identify the man by race. He says, 'The one who had mercy on him.' Jesus' question was designed to cause the lawyer to consider the personal side of the story. The story was not just a question of right or wrong, it was a question that penetrates the heart. Can you see what Jesus was doing? By reversing the way this story was being viewed, Jesus changes both the question and the answer. He distinguishes labeling people *neighbors* based on their proximity from labeling them based on the kind of people they are.[69] By making the Samaritan the example, Jesus points out that neighbors may come in all shapes, sizes, and packages. Neighbors are not limited to the family next door or to the people we know and like. Neighbors can be anyone we come in contact with and those people whom we have an opportunity to influence.

Professor David E. Garland of Southern Baptist Theological Seminary makes an important point that many people choose to overlook or ignore. "It is an inconvenient truth that ultimately we will be responsible for, and it has to do with Jesus expanding the definition of your neighbor." Garland rightly claims that Jesus expands the definition of neighbor "to include those whom we would write

---

68   *Merriam-Webster's Dictionary*, s.v. "Samaritan."
69   Darrell L. Bock, *The NIV Application Commentary: Luke*, 301.

off as enemies."[70] Jesus has a way of taking spiritual concepts and turning our world upside down. In the story of the Good Samaritan, He reminds us we are all connected to each other by virtue of being members of the human race. Who is our neighbor? From God's perspective our neighbor is the person we have an opportunity to influence and interact with.

How Do I Love My Neighbor?

Jesus never leaves us where He finds us; He takes us with Him on the journey. Here Jesus sheds light on what our love is supposed to look like.

> So he went to him and bandaged his wounds, pouring on oil and wine; and he set him on his own animal, brought him to an inn, and took care of him. On the next day, when he departed, he took out two denarii, gave them to the innkeeper, and said to him, "Take care of him; and whatever more you spend, when I come again, I will repay you."[71]

Jesus uses all kinds of verbs to describe how active this person was in ministering to his newly discovered neighbor. But the bottom line was, the Samarian took the time and money and invested in him. What are some of the considerations?

- He was concerned over his injuries and bandaged him up.
- He was concerned over his circumstance and brought him to an inn.
- He was concerned over his future and made provisions.

---

[70] Garland, *The NIV Application Commentary: Mark,* 485.
[71] Luke 10:34–35 (NKJV).

The level of concern demonstrated by the Samaritan and the actions he took exceeded everyone's expectations. It demonstrates if we really become interested in influencing people for Christ, exceeding their expectations is a good start. When we exceed the expectation of other people, it is a sure way to capture their attention. People are more likely to respond to circumstances where one has displayed concern, rather than a show of words or a pledge of good intentions.

Concern Demonstrated

Alfred Edmond was stuck in Overland Park, Kansas. His motorcycle had run out of gas, and Edmond had run out of money after a long trip from Las Cruces, New Mexico. He was just fourteen miles from his destination of Olathe, Kansas, where he was supposed to have an important job interview. Things were beginning to fall apart for Alfred when all of a sudden he met Overland Park police sergeant Dan Carney. Carney pulled up in his squad car and asked Edmond if there was a problem. After Alfred explained his circumstances to Sergeant Carney, Carney handed Alfred eight dollars to fill the tank in his motorcycle and then drove away. Alfred wrote down Sergeant Carney's name, but somewhere along the way, he lost the piece of paper.

Fast forward twenty-one years. One day Alfred stumbled across that old piece of paper with Sergeant Carney's name on it, and he decided to send his Good Samaritan an eight-dollar money order with a note thanking him for his help in a time of great need. When Dan Carney received the money order and correspondence, he said, "Unbelievable. One little comment or a little thing here or there can mean so much to somebody. That's wonderful."[72]

---

[72]   Sermon Illustrations, *Preaching Today*, accessed July 16, 2014, http://preachingtoday.com.

Every situation we will encounter will be a little bit different, but I'm convinced God directs our paths and He places us in ministry opportunities. Our main responsibility as a neighbor is to be sensitive to the guidance of the Holy Spirit in our interactions and to respond appropriately. I've mentioned earlier God will not allow our hurts or disappointments in life to be wasted. He uses our experiences and our humanity as examples and lessons to encourage others. God has designed and wired us in such a way as to make us be codependent upon one another. We are going to feel a greater sense of purpose when God blends our lives with people who are facing similar obstacles.

When we encounter people who are facing similar challenges, that encounter creates a connection between us. It develops a trust that breaks down barriers and builds bridges. It allows us to become the salt and light of the world that Jesus spoke of in His Sermon on the Mount. In life we are always building either bridges or walls. When we build bridges of faith, we are in a sense laying up our treasures in heaven. We are demonstrating ourselves to be true neighbors to other people. Who is my neighbor? Well, it's anyone you come in contact with! Anyone whom you have an opportunity to influence.

CHAPTER ELEVEN

Taking Ownership of Your Life

I once spoke to a financial adviser about plans for the future after my retirement from the government at the age of fifty-six. It was too soon for social security, Medicare, and other benefits to be factored in for my situation. Therefore other factors had to be considered. He made this comment to me during our conversation: "Keith, if we lived with expiration dates—like milk, bread, and other grocery products—planning for the future would be easy." I began to think about what he had said, and a scripture verse from Hebrews 9 came to mind. "It is appointed unto men to die once, but after this the judgment."[73] The truth is, in reality, we do live with expiration dates, but it is only God who knows them. If God tarries, every person that has ever lived will one day reach his or her own personal expiration date. Whether we die naturally or as the result of an accident or God calls us home through some type of supernatural process, our time

---

[73]   Hebrews 9:27 (NKJV).

on earth is limited and will expire. No one escapes the brevity of life; it is part of the natural process of God's plan. The fact that death is universal and we traditionally have little impact on determining the exact date that life will end suggests the sovereignty of God.

God initiated life in the beginning, and He created each individual life with a purpose. "For I know the plans I have for you," declares the LORD, "plans to prosper you and not to harm you, plans to give you hope and a future."[74] When our life's plan has run its course, or through a series of circumstances our life ends prematurely (at least from our point of view), what awaits us is accountability. To use an old accounting term we might call it a reckoning. A reckoning occurs when the life books of God are balanced and everything that affects life is taken into consideration. Our life will be reviewed, evaluated, and a judgment rendered based on our stewardship of life. The Bible clearly talks about two types of judgments that will await every single person who has ever lived following the expiration date.

Each person will stand before one of two final judgments. When everything in our lives is analyzed and our life's plan is made public, we will give an account of our conduct, behavior, or attitude and our actions before one of these judgment seats of Christ. The first of the judgments spoken of in the Bible is the Great White Throne Judgment. This is the judgment of the unrighteous dead from the beginning of time. The second judgment is what is known as the Bema Judgment Seat of Christ. This is a judgment of the righteous dead, and it will occur separately from the Great White Throne Judgment. We will talk more about the Bema Judgment in a moment; let's first look at the Great White Throne Judgment so that we can develop an understanding of what it deals with.

---

[74]   Jeremiah 29:11 (NIV).

The Great White Throne Judgment (Unrighteous Dead)

In the Book of Revelation we are told of The Great White Throne Judgment:

> Then I saw a great white throne and Him who sat on it, from whose face the earth and the heaven fled away. And there was found no place for them.
>
> And I saw the dead, small and great, standing before God, and books were opened. And another book was opened, which is [the Book] of Life. And the dead were judged according to their works, by the things which were written in the books.
>
> The sea gave up the dead who were in it, and Death and Hades delivered up the dead who were in them. And they were judged, each one according to his works.
>
> Then Death and Hades were cast into the lake of fire. This is the second death.
>
> And anyone not found written in the Book of Life was cast into the lake of fire.[75]

The Great White Throne Judgment represents the final judgment at the conclusion of human history. It occurs just prior to the beginning of all eternal life. There are many references to a throne in the Book of Revelation and in this context it illustrates a place where God sits and orchestrates the activities of heaven. One commentator mentions that nearly fifty times in Revelation the word *throne* is used to denote a place where God's presence is central to the activities. In

---

[75]   Revelation 20:11–15 (NKJV).

this case, the activity is judgment. I would like to call several things to your attention in Revelation 20 verses 11–15:

- First, the corruption and contamination of the earth and heaven (the world system) is banished from sight; the Bible says "they fled away." This describes the situation that exists today in our physical and economic world. Even though we refer to things being permanent, the truth is, in reality, everything is temporary. Time is like a huge universal clock representing mankind, that eventually winds down and stops. One day everything we have invested our lives into—our work, our possessions, and our plans—will vanish. This is what we see happening today; there is nothing that we are currently involved with, with the exception of our soul, that is of a permanent nature.

- Second, we see all the unrighteous dead awaiting judgment gathered together. The purpose of the Great White Throne Judgment is to judge the lives of those who have died separated from Christ. This includes, but is not limited to, the rich, the poor, the notable, the forgotten, the influential, the beggar, and everyone from every social, cultural, and economic diversification of people that has ever existed. All are gathered for the purpose of standing before God and having their individual life judged. If there is one great consolation for people who cry out for justice, they will be presenting their case before the fairest, the most just, and the most honest "Judge" they could ever appear before, Jesus Christ, and their case will be correctly judged.

- Third, we see "the Books" are opened. The Books represent the ledger of human activity regarding each and every person that has lived since Adam and Eve. In the Gospel account of Jesus's ministry in the Book of Matthew, He

made a reference to "every jot and tittle." This was a reference to the smallest letter and the smallest marking in the
Hebrew language, and the point Jesus is making is nothing
will be overlooked in the final judgment. We are told "the
dead were judged according to their works, by the things
written in the books."

- Fourth, the second book, the "Book of Life," is absolutely
the most critical part of this judgment. When the Book
of Life is opened, it represents the final scan for the righteousness of the human soul on each individual person
who has ever lived. The Bible says, "Anyone not found
written in the Book of Life was cast into the lake of fire."
There will be no excuses, there will be no pardons, there
will be no amnesty; judgment will be rendered, and the
sentence will be handed down.

Guilty, But Not Guilty

A few years ago I was on my way to work one morning around
seven, and as I was driving to work, the most direct route carried me
through a school zone. The school had classes that began at eight
thirty, so there was very little activity as I passed by. The speed limit
in the area is normally thirty-five miles an hour, except for times des-
ignated on the school sign. The speed limit is then reduced to fifteen
miles per hour. As I passed the school, I was not paying attention to
the reduced speed limit and failed to make adequate reductions to my
speed. I noticed at the end of the school zone only one person standing beside their car. It was a police officer, and he was waving me over
to the side of the road. Having been a police officer myself a number
of years before, I felt that providing a reasonable explanation and
apologizing, accompanied by a promise to pay closer attention to the
speed limit, might get me a warning ticket. I was wrong! The officer
came up to the window of my car and asked, "Where are you going

in such a hurry?" I responded in my most sincere tone, "Officer, thirty-five isn't a hurry to anywhere!" He said, "It is here!" and he took my license and proceeded to write me a ticket. Needless to say, that incident took only ten minutes, but it ruined my whole day. This was the first ticket that I had received since being a teenager, so I decided to get a copy of my driving record (which happened to be spotless thanks to God's grace) and appear in court before the judge. As my court day approached, I began to think more and more about what I would say to the judge. The only thing I could think of that sounded plausible was a request for mercy, perhaps a Prayer for Judgment, the legal term for mercy. Mercy is the act of withholding what a person truly deserves, and that's exactly what I wanted. It was unreasonable to think that I could be "not guilty," unless I thought I could get off on a technicality, because I was, in fact, guilty as charged.

My reckoning day arrived, and when I went into the courtroom, I was surprised at what I saw. The judge presiding that day was someone whom I had known during my years in law enforcement. He had been a local attorney in private practice during my tenure as a police officer. I knew him to be a person of great respect and reputation, a morally just individual. When my case was called before the court by the district attorney, he read the charges as I stood before the judge. The judge looked at me directly and addressed me personally by name and asked me how I've been doing. I said, "Fine," and then he asked, "What can I do for you?" I said, "I would like to request a Prayer for Judgment!" Seeing the paper in my hand, he asked, "Is that your driving record?" I said, "Yes, sir." He said, "Let me take a look at it." As he examined the details of my record, after a few moments he grabbed his gavel and banged it on the bench and said, "Granted!" The judge allowed my Prayer for Judgment. He treated me with special favor in the eyes of the law by dispensing both grace and mercy: grace by giving me something I did not deserve and mercy by withholding what I did deserve. I was treated as if the offense never occurred. The Prayer for Judgment prevented any negative judicial consequences that would normally accompany a guilty plea. It wiped the slate clean. It reminded me of the judicial process of my being made guiltless by knowing Christ, the Judge.

The Bema Judgment (The Righteous Dead)

I have heard a number of Christians innocently say, "If I can only get to heaven, I'm not going to worry about anything else! Jesus will take care of everything." This type of spiritual thinking represents a shallow understanding of how the Christian life is to be lived. If the major concern is "getting my ticket punched to heaven," then we have some spiritual digging to do in order to get to biblical truth. The danger with this type of thinking is it fails to incorporate God's overall plan for humanity. It overlooks the primary purpose of "what" and "why" and "for what purpose do we exist?"

The Bible is clear; God designed the Christian life to be a reflection of His glory. One of the main themes of Christianity is to love God and to love others, to serve God and to serve others. As recipients of God's grace, we are called to dispense His grace and His mercy by serving others. This provides the opportunity to influence the world for Christ and make a difference by taking on the metaphorical characteristics of salt and light. Salt flavors and preserves; light illuminates and disinfects. When we serve God's purposes, we become His preservative and His light to others.

Another way of looking at our responsibilities to others is by seeing our role as spiritual stewards. A steward in New Testament times was one employed on a large estate to manage domestic concerns of the owner, in other words, one who oversees or manages affairs in another's absence. As Christians, if we are to be like Christ, we should seek ways we can be of service to others and manage our lives in a way that brings honor to God. One of the great blessings of serving God is the promise that one day God will evaluate the level of service that has been rendered and reward the faithfulness of believers.

This evaluation, or this judgment, is referred to as the Bema Judgment. *Bema* is the Greek word used for *rewards*, and this word was adopted from Greek athletic contests, specifically the Isthmian games, where the contestants would compete for the prize under the careful scrutiny of judges who would then make sure that every rule of the contest was obeyed. The victor of a given event, who participated according to the rules, was led by the judge to the platform called the bema. There the laurel wreath was placed on his or her head as a symbol of victory.[76] This account provides a wonderful picture of what takes place in the lives of Christians when they stand at the Judgment Seat of Christ. The Apostle Paul refers to the Judgment Seat of Christ on several different occasions in the New Testament. In one particular passage he describes what takes place. Paul says,

> Therefore we make it our aim, whether present or absent, to be well pleasing to Him. For we must all appear before the judgment seat of Christ, that each one may receive the things done in the body, according to what he has done, whether good or bad. Knowing, therefore, the terror of the Lord, we persuade men; but we are well known to God, and I also trust are well known in your conscience.[77]

The Apostle Paul is seeking to encourage believers to be faithful in their witness and service by saying, "Make it our aim, whether

---

[76] "The Doctrine of Rewards: The Judgment Seat (Bema) of Christ," Bible.org, accessed March 20, 2015, https://bible.org/article/doctrine-rewards-judgment-seat-bema-christ.

[77] 2 Corinthians 5:9–11 (NKJV).

present or absent, to be well pleasing to Him [Christ]." Then he goes on to explain why this is so important in the life of the Christian: "We must all appear before the judgment seat of Christ that each one [each believer] may receive the things done in the body." This is a spiritual assessment of our stewardship and our faithfulness to Christ. At the risk of sounding redundant, the Judgment Seat of Christ is a rewards ceremony for faithfulness, not a punishment. If there is any sadness present at the Bema Judgment, it would only be the realization of leaving rewards on the table and falling short of our potential. In other words, not receiving all of the spiritual rewards that were within our grasp.

The question that might develop in our minds is, How would we know? Honestly, this may be difficult to discern without a high level of spiritual sensitivity. It seems to me the only safe bet is to be continually faithful and ask for God's unfailing guidance. If we seek to be in the center of God's will each and every day and we are faithful, it would be hard to imagine leaving behind any of God's spiritual rewards. In closing, the Bible does mention five Crowns as rewards for the believer:

1. The Incorruptible Crown (1 Corinthians 9:25)
2. The Crown of Righteousness (2 Timothy 4:8)
3. The Crown of Life (Revelation 2:10)
4. The Crown of Glory (1 Peter 5:4)
5. The Crown of Rejoicing (1 Thessalonians 2:19)

CHAPTER TWELVE

Making Your Life Count

Decisions

Every day we are faced with hundreds of decisions. Every time we pull up to something as simple as an intersection, we are faced with decisions. Go right, go left, or go straight; one way represents the best way to our destination. One way may carry us farther from our destination; one way may eventually get us there, but we may have to alter our schedule. One way allows us to get to our destination within our original parameters. There is really only one *best* way to get to our intended destination.

Poet Robert Frost provides a perspective on making choices in a poem titled "The Road Not Taken."

Two roads diverged in a yellow wood,
And sorry I could not travel both
And be one traveler, long I stood
And looked down one as far as I could
To where it bent in the undergrowth;

Then took the other, as just as fair,
And having perhaps the better claim,
Because it was grassy and wanted wear;
Though as for that the passing there
Had worn them really about the same,

And both that morning equally lay
In leaves no step had trodden black.
Oh, I kept the first for another day!
Yet knowing how way leads on to way,
I doubted if I should ever come back.

I shall be telling this with a sigh
Somewhere ages and ages hence:
Two roads diverged in a wood, and I--
I took the one less traveled by,
And that has made all the difference.[78]

Many factors affect the decisions we make, but we must remember we can decide on only one road at a time and only one way is best. When making decisions, we might consider a parable Jesus shared of the Two Foundations. As a master teacher, Jesus spent the majority of His ministry preaching and teaching about the Kingdom of Heaven. His goal was to show how we are to respond to the spiritual light that we've been given. His methods were not coercive, nor were they threatening. They were informative and insightful and designed to prompt our thinking and elicit a response. The simple definition of *parable* is an "earthly story with a heavenly meaning,"

---

[78] Robert Frost, "The Road Not Taken," Poets.org, accessed March 20, 2015 http://www.poets.org/poetsorg/poem/road-not-taken.

and parables were an effective way for Him to give spiritual insight for our earthly decisions.

The Parable of the Two Foundations

The Parable of the Two Foundations is found in Luke 6:46–49, and it provides insight into making decisions based on logical reasoning. The background of this parable comes on the heels of Jesus teaching about the Kingdom of God. When Jesus finishes His discourse, He shares the Parable of the Two Foundations, and there are three notable themes that emerge that become the basis for decision-making:

1. Who is Lord?
2. Who is wise?
3. Who is foolish?

Who is Lord?

> But why do you call Me "Lord, Lord," and not do the things which I say? Whoever comes to Me, and hears My sayings and does them, I will show you whom he is like:[79]

Jesus asked the question, "But why do you call Me 'Lord, Lord,' and not do the things which I say?" The reference to Jesus as "Lord" from Jesus's standpoint was more than something to be used as a complimentary title. From a Kingdom perspective it suggests a willingness or desire to follow in obedience. It elevated Jesus beyond the position of simply being a teacher to an authoritative position of a person who decides things, one who has subjects under his authority,

---

[79]   Luke 4:46–47 (NKJV).

like a ruler or monarch. His question was designed to stimulate their thinking and to prompt their hearts toward obedience. It was not enough to simply call someone "Lord" without having an attitude of service because that would only translate as lip service. The point Jesus was making, to call someone "Lord," should be a call to action. A faithful believer is not one who tells others how to live; it's one who actually lives belief out for others to see. Not professors of the faith, but possessors of the faith. In other words, it is when *our actions speak louder than words*!

Intention Over Action

Since the 1940s, the Ad Council has been the leading producer of public service announcements, and of the thousands of commercials they have produced, their work for the Don't Almost Give campaign has been particularly powerful. One ad shows a man with crutches struggling to go up a flight of concrete stairs. The narrator says, "This is a man who almost learned to walk at a rehab center that almost got built by people who almost gave money." After a brief pause, the announcer continues: "Almost gave. How good is *almost* giving? About as good as *almost* walking."

Another excerpt shows a homeless man curled up in a ball on a pile of rags. One ratty bedsheet shields him from the cold. The narrator says, "This is Jack Thomas. Today someone almost brought Jack something to eat. Someone almost brought him to a shelter. And someone else almost brought him a warm blanket." After a brief pause, the narrator continues: "And Jack Thomas? Well, he *almost* made it through the night."

Another segment shows an older woman sitting alone in a room, staring out a window. The narrator says, "This is Sarah Watkins. A lot of people almost helped her. One almost cooked for her. Another almost drove her to the doctor. Still another almost stopped by to say hello. They *almost* helped. They *almost* gave of themselves. But *almost* giving is the same as not giving at all."

Each ad ends with a simple, direct message: "Don't almost give. Give."[80]

Jesus says, "Whoever comes to Me, and hears My sayings and does them, I will show you whom he is like:"

Who Is Wise?

> He is like a man building a house, who dug deep and laid the foundation on the rock. And when the flood arose, the stream beat vehemently against that house, and could not shake it, for it was founded on the rock.[81]

The wise builder is the man who thought through the process and acted on solid information. To be described as wise means *one who is supplied with information and makes informed, good-sense decisions based on the insight one has been given.*

One of the wonderful things about Christianity is its basis in truth. Christianity doesn't ask you to throw out your common sense in preference to faith. Faith is not a blind leap in the dark; faith is based on the evidences that we are surrounded by, particularly those of conscience and nature. Faith is based in truth and complements common sense and facts. Evidence also includes, not excludes, the Bible. Truth establishes reason, and reason works to build faith. In this particular parable, Jesus shares that the wise man was smart

---

80   Ted De Hass, Bedford, Iowa, and Brian Lowery, managing editor, *PreachingToday.com; source: YouTube.com* (Ad #1 [man on crutches]; Ad #2 [homeless man]; Ad #3 [older woman]. *Online accessed 3/6/2015.*

81   Luke 6:48 (NKJV).

enough and reasonable enough to know the best foundation would be the sturdiness of a rock. A rock is lasting, strong, sure, and able to endure even in many different types of weather. Jesus said, "When the flood arose, the stream beat vehemently against that house, and could not shake it." *What a wonderful picture of faith in Christ this is.* I do not know of anyone who has not had at least one or two severe storms to hit during a lifetime. It could be the loss of a job, a report of terminal cancer, or the loss of a child. Storms can and do happen in people's lives every day, and they seem to come at the worst possible time. Jesus finishes His illustration of the wise man by saying, "The stream beat vehemently against that house, and could not shake it, for *it was founded on the rock.*"

Every person will eventually encounter a storm. My own experience has carried me through a few storms in my lifetime, and the major thing I had to hold onto was my faith in Christ, at a time when everything else seemed insufficient, my accomplishments, my education, my experience. But, dear friend, I am here to tell you, if faith is all you have left to hold onto, that's enough! Because faith is *"founded on the rock, Jesus Christ."*

The third point that Jesus makes in this parable is the second option, an alternative choice referred to as the foolish choice. The foolish choice is one that is made on a daily basis by people who have short-range goals or people who are looking for a quick fix. People who normally engage in making foolish choices are people who put a premium on factors like convenience, desires, emotions, and personal investments of time. This is not to say that some of these factors should not be considered at times; it is simply saying these factors should not be the driver of our choices. These factors are considered to be temporary in nature and ultimately have a short life span or endurance level.

Who Is Foolish?

> But he who heard and did nothing is like a man
> who built a house on the earth without a founda-
> tion, against which the stream beat vehemently;
> and immediately it fell. And the ruin of that
> house was great.[82]

The "foolish" builder is the man who built his house without a foundation. The Book of Matthew in the New Testament refers to the foundation as being "sand" and describes a foundation that will not last. The word *foolish* actually refers to a lack of judgment, to relying on ridiculously unreasonable or unsound practices. Investing in something that doesn't last can fall into the category of being foolish.[83]

Several years ago my wife and I went to the beach, and we were sitting under an umbrella, just watching people build sand castles or make impressions in the sand. After an hour or so a group of young people about ten or eleven of them around college age came out to the beach with their shovels, their buckets, and other utility equipment. They began to build a fortress complete with places to sit and lounge, a retaining wall, and a gateway. It was massive and very impressive. They spent several hours constructing this tremendous fort, and we watched with interest as they sat around enjoying themselves for about thirty minutes.

Shortly the tide began to push back against the shoreline, and as it did, the young people left. My wife and I watched as the surf pounded against the fortress. Within minutes the fortress had fallen, and you could no longer tell there had ever been any activity on the

---

82   Luke 6:49 (NKJV).
83   *Merriam-Webster's Dictionary*, s.v. "foolish."

beach. The sand and the fortress had been no match for the strength and power of the ocean and its waves. Even without a storm, the efforts of the young people had only a temporary impact on the beach, and that impact lasted only thirty minutes. Today people build their hopes and careers on the foundation of the world, a world system that we know will one day not be able to support itself and will collapse, according to what the Bible says.

- The political world doesn't have the answers! Politicians are leading taxpayers deeper and deeper in debt, at the same time promising things they cannot possibly provide.
- The economic and financial world doesn't have the answers! There is so much greed and corruption that is so pervasive the monetary foundation of the world is shaky at best, with many governments already defaulting on what they owe to each other.
- The judicial world doesn't have the answers! Many decisions are being handled by courts based on societal and cultural preferences. When the government decides what laws are enforced and which ones are ignored, when the Constitution and Bill of Rights, founding documents of our society, become fluid rather than foundational, it signals the beginning stages of a society that is unraveling.

According to the Bible, the foolish, or the unwise, builder is the one who heard and did nothing. Most people think they have plenty of time to make decisions. There is no real sense of urgency, so many procrastinate. I would like to remind you of an event that happened on September 11, 2001, where nearly three thousand people went to work that morning expecting it to be no different than any other day. However, that day they would not return home. That day happened to be their final day on earth, and no one knew it until after the fact.

Life has no real guarantees. The Bible teaches us our lives on earth are temporary. The Book of James states, "It's only a vapor," then it is gone. We know the truth of that statement because we know the reality of life and death. No one physically lives forever. Humanity has been cursed with death, but the Bible teaches of a spiritual existence that continues on after physical death. The teachings of Jesus have stood the test of time, and they have proven to be true and accurate. Jesus provided parables in order to engage our minds and encourage us to use our reason, as it relates to eternity.

Jesus also gave us the two things that matter most, His greatest teaching!

Then one of the scribes came, and having heard them reasoning together, perceiving that He had answered them well, asked Him, "Which is the first commandment of all?"

> Jesus answered him, "The first of all the commandments is: 'Hear, O Israel, the LORD our God, the LORD is one. And you shall love the LORD your God with all your heart, with all your soul, with all your mind, and with all your strength.' This is the first commandment. And the second, like it, is this: 'You shall love your neighbor as yourself.' There is no other commandment greater than these."
>
> So the scribe said to Him, "Well said, Teacher. You have spoken the truth, for there is one God, and there is no other but He. And to love Him with all the heart, with all the understanding, with all the soul, and with all the strength, and to love one's neighbor as oneself, is more than all the whole burnt offerings and sacrifices."

Now when Jesus saw that he answered wisely, He said to him, "You are not far from the kingdom of God!"

The decision is up to us; we choose. Each person's eternity is based on a decision that person will make about Christ. It is a personal choice each individual will make. If anyone is coerced into making a decision, it invalidates choice and free will. Choice and free will are important options regarding worship and adoration. Jesus said in chapter 22 of Revelation: "I, Jesus have sent My angel to testify to you these things in the churches. I am the Root and the Offspring of David, the Bright and Morning Star. And the Spirit and the bride say, 'Come!' And let him who hears say, 'Come!' And let him who thirsts come, whoever desires, let him take the water of life freely."

Jesus offers an invitation, but each individual must make his or her own personal decision. If today you desire to make a decision to surrender your life to Christ, it is as simple as repeating this prayer!

Dear gracious and merciful God,

I know that I'm a sinner and unrighteous before You. But I believe that Jesus Christ, the righteous, died for my sins. I accept by faith and, on the authority of the Word of God, His sacrifice and His redemptive work on the Cross, and I ask for Your forgiveness! I believe and acknowledge, based on my faith in Him, that I will one day live eternally in heaven. I ask for Your blessing and Your Spirit to dwell in me and guide me in this present life until one day You call me home. I ask this in the name of my Lord and Savior, Jesus Christ! Amen.

CHAPTER THIRTEEN

The New You

New Steps in Christ

When we make a decision to follow Christ, we face questions about how to start, and what are the best practices? I have made a list of five things I believe are essential in developing a life of faith in Christ and finding purpose in life.

1. *Be thankful and grateful and acknowledge God each day.* Living each day with a thankful heart toward God has many internal and external benefits. Contentment and appreciation are two of the most important stress relievers a person can possess. Studies show that people who are thankful live longer, happier lives!

2. *Pray for spiritual insight.* God enters our lives through invitation. If you pray for God's direction and understanding, He is faithful and will open up opportunities to grow your faith. Every time Jesus needed spiritual help, He prayed, and God answered. God does the same thing for believers today. We speak to God in prayer and give Him permission

to have His way in our lives. He speaks to us through His Word, through local Bible studies, printed devotionals, or a word from a friend. The bottom line is God is faithful and responds to our request. Jesus said, "God would not leave us as orphans."

3. *Find and belong to a Bible-believing church or fellowship.* Becoming a part of a Bible-believing church or fellowship is essential to spiritual development and Christian growth. Jesus gave birth to the church for a reason, because there is strength in numbers. God has gifted everyone with a spiritual gift (at least one) designed to be used within the body of believers in order to build them up. Our task is to find the right church and discover our gift(s) so they can be utilized for the glory of God.

4. *Seek to know God better.* The Bible says, "Study to show yourself approved." Read and independently study the Bible. I am often asked which Bible is best. I normally reply, "The one you'll read!" There are many good translations for you to consider. I personally prefer the NKJV with a study commentary. Unless you read Hebrew, Greek, or Aramaic, everything available to you will be a translation. It is important to choose a translation that speaks clearly to you, so be willing to invest a little research. I would avoid paraphrased versions, though. Paraphrasing can possibly edit important details out of a passage. When you're reading a love letter from your best friend, you want to see all the details they include, and the Bible is God's love letter to mankind. You will want to see all the details. If you are ambitious, you may want to have several different versions available. I love comparing the text of different versions like the ESV, NIV, KJV, and the NKJV.

Comparing the texts allows me to come away feeling that I have the best interpretation of what the text says.

5. *Witness.* The greatest tool you have in your spiritual tool-shed is your witness for Christ. People can argue the Bible, they can argue Jesus, but they cannot argue what Jesus has done for you. Your witness is highly individualistic, and you own it. Nobody has your personal witness because it belongs to you. People may not like your witness, but they cannot argue its authenticity.

May God richly bless you as you serve Him!

Enthusiastically His,
Keith Gardner

Survey Results of "Important Life Considerations"

Disclaimer: Three hundred and twenty-seven people covering a broad spectrum of the population participated in this survey. Demographic questions 12–15 were not available to all participants.

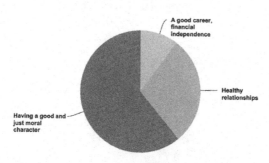

Q1 **What do you consider to be the most important pursuit in life?**

Answered: 323   Skipped: 4

Answer Choices	Responses	
A good career, financial independence	10.22%	33
Popularity, fame, notoriety	0.00%	0
Healthy relationships	28.79%	93
Having a good and just moral character	60.99%	197
Total		323

Q2 When it comes to activities that you participate in, as a matter of self evaluation, would you consider your role to be:

Answered: 325   Skipped: 2

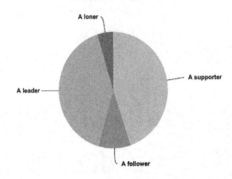

Answer Choices	Responses	
A supporter	44.92%	146
A follower	9.54%	31
A leader	40.92%	133
A loner	4.62%	15
Total		325

Q3 On a scale of 1 to 10, with 1 being the least important and 10 being the most important, how important is it to you to leave a legacy to others?

Answered: 325   Skipped: 2

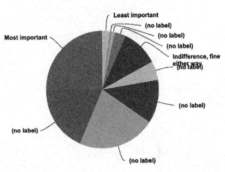

	Least important	(no label)	(no label)	(no label)	Indifference, fine either way	(no label)	(no label)	(no label)	(no label)	Most important	Total	Weighted Average
(no label)	2.15%	0.62%	0.92%	3.08%	10.46%	5.23%	12.00%	22.15%	18.46%	24.92%		
	7	2	3	10	34	17	39	72	60	81	325	7.79

THE TWO THINGS THAT MATTER MOST

Q4 What do you consider to be the strongest influence in your life?

Answered: 325   Skipped: 2

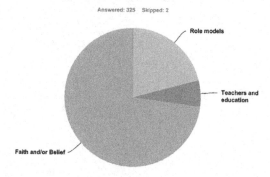

Answer Choices	Responses	
Role models	20.92%	68
Teachers and education	6.15%	20
Faith and/or Belief	72.92%	237
Government and Government Programs	0.00%	0
Total		325

Q5 If you were to look back on your life today, regardless of age, and evaluate your personal satisfaction with what you have accomplished, would you say you:

Answered: 325   Skipped: 2

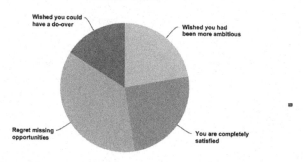

Answer Choices	Responses	
Wished you had been more ambitious	22.15%	72
You are completely satisfied	25.23%	82
Regret missing opportunities	36.62%	119
Wished you could have a do-over	16.00%	52
Total		325

Q6 If you could give advice to someone on making their life count based on your own experience, would you advise them to:

Answered: 325 Skipped: 2

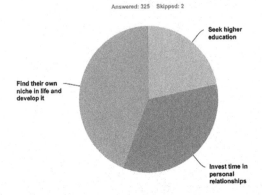

Answer Choices	Responses	
Seek higher education	21.85%	71
Invest time in personal relationships	34.15%	111
Find their own niche in life and develop it	44.00%	143
Seek out Government Aid or assistance	0.00%	0
Total		325

Q7 The average life span is 28,472 days, or roughly about 78 years. Do you consider that to be:

Answered: 327 Skipped: 0

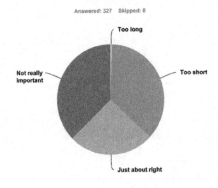

Answer Choices	Responses	
Too long	0.61%	2
Too short	36.39%	119
Just about right	25.69%	84
Not really important	37.31%	122
Total		327

THE TWO THINGS THAT MATTER MOST

Q8 When considering your own personal conviction concerning the origin of life, would you say that you believe:

Answered: 324   Skipped: 3

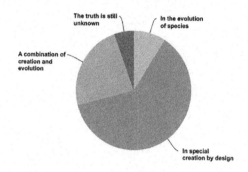

Answer Choices	Responses	
In the evolution of species	8.95%	29
In special creation by design	62.04%	201
A combination of creation and evolution	23.46%	76
The truth is still unknown	5.56%	18
Total		324

Q9 Based on your life experience, what human emotion do you consider to be the strongest or the most dominate that a person can experience?

Answered: 324   Skipped: 3

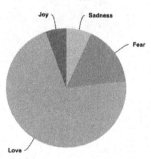

Answer Choices	Responses	
Sadness	6.79%	22
Fear	16.36%	53
Love	71.30%	231
Joy	5.56%	18
Total		324

Q10 Would you consider your outlook on life to be:

Answered: 326   Skipped: 1

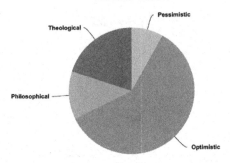

Answer Choices	Responses	
Pessimistic	8.28%	27
Optimistic	59.51%	194
Philosophical	12.27%	40
Theological	19.94%	65
Total		326

Q12 Age

Answered: 69   Skipped: 258

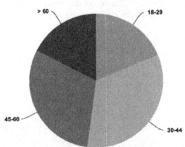

Answer Choices	Responses	
< 18	0.00%	0
18-29	18.84%	13
30-44	33.33%	23
45-60	30.43%	21
> 60	17.39%	12
Total		69

THE TWO THINGS THAT MATTER MOST

Q13 Household Income

Answered: 69   Skipped: 256

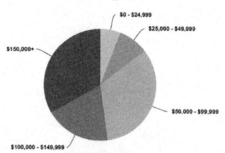

Answer Choices	Responses	
$0 - $24,999	5.80%	4
$25,000 - $49,999	8.70%	6
$50,000 - $99,999	33.33%	23
$100,000 - $149,999	18.84%	13
$150,000+	33.33%	23
Total		69

Q14 Education

Answered: 68   Skipped: 259

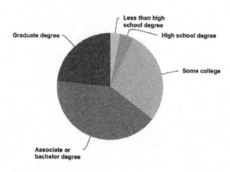

Answer Choices	Responses	
Less than high school degree	2.94%	2
High school degree	4.41%	3
Some college	27.94%	19
Associate or bachelor degree	41.18%	28
Graduate degree	23.53%	16
Total		68

Q15 Location (Census Region)

Answered: 68   Skipped: 259

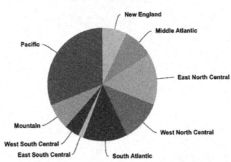

Answer Choices	Responses	
New England	7.35%	5
Middle Atlantic	8.82%	6
East North Central	14.71%	10
West North Central	11.76%	8
South Atlantic	13.24%	9
East South Central	1.47%	1
West South Central	4.41%	3
Mountain	7.35%	5
Pacific	30.88%	21
Total		68

Appendix B

Research Questions

1. On a scale of 1 to 10, with 1 being the least important and 10 being the most important, how important to you do you consider having a legacy to be?

2. When it comes to activities that you participate in, as a matter of self-evaluation, what would you consider your role to be?
   (A) A supporter
   (B) A follower
   (C) A leader
   (D) A loner

3. What do you consider to be the most important pursuit in life?
   (A) A good career, financial independence
   (B) Popularity, fame, notoriety
   (C) Relationships
   (D) Moral or just character

4. What do you consider to be the strongest influence in your life?
   (A) Role models
   (B) Teachers or education
   (C) Faith or belief
   (D) Government programs

5. If you were to look back on your life today, regardless of age, and evaluate your satisfaction with what you have accomplished, you would say that you
   (A) wished that you had been more ambitious.
   (B) are completely satisfied.
   (C) regret missing opportunities.
   (D) wished that you could have a do-over.

6. If you could give advice to someone about making their life count based on your own experience, what would you advise them to do?
   (A) Seek higher education.
   (B) Invest time in personal relationships.
   (C) Find their own niche in life and develop it.
   (D) Seek out government aid or assistance.

7. The average life span is 28,472 days, or roughly about 78 years, on average. Do you consider that to be
   (A) too long?
   (B) too short?
   (C) just about right?
   (D) not really important?

8. When considering the origin of life, my own personal conviction is that life originated with
   (A) the evolution of species.

(B) special creation by design.

(C) a combination of creation and evolution.

(D) The truth is still unknown.

9. Based on your life experience, what human emotion do you consider to be the strongest or the most dominate emotion a person can experience?

(A) Sadness

(B) Fear

(C) Anger

(D) Love

(E) Joy

10. What would you consider your outlook on life to be?

(A) Pessimistic

(B) Optimistic

(C) Philosophical

(D) Theological

Keith R. Gardner is pastor of First Free Will Baptist Church in Greenville, North Carolina, where he has served the past four years. Prior to ministry he served five years as a law enforcement officer and nearly thirty years as a manager with the US Postal Service. He graduated from Liberty University and holds three advanced degrees from Liberty Baptist Theological Seminary, a Master of Arts in Religion, Master of Divinity and a Doctor of Ministry degree. He is teaching community Bible classes and has written and published *Effective Transitional Ministry Plan, Pastoral Leadership in the 21st Century Church, Effective Transitional Ministry, Why We Say No, When God Says Go*, and numerous articles for the Layman's League, a denominational men's outreach. He and his wife, Sheryl, have a daughter and two sons and three precious grandchildren. The Gardners live in Greenville, North Carolina.

CPSIA information can be obtained
at www.ICGtesting.com
Printed in the USA
BVOW03s1857170717

489519BV00001B/60/P